Jewish Cooking

FROM

Around the World

Josephine Levy Bacon

To Mrs. Esther Levy and all those unsung Jewish heroines whose efforts in the kitchen have for so long been taken for granted.

The author would like to acknowledge the help of Vanessa Vasey, Kate Evelyn Hackman, Hannah Levy, and Bruce Johnson, without whose encouragement this book would never have been written. She would also like to thank the London Board of Shechita, the Kashrus Commission, and the London Beth Din for their assistance.

Photographic credits

Color photographs: Matthew Klein
Food Styling: Andrea Swenson
Photo styling: Linda Cheverton

Jacket and cover design: Milton Glaser, Inc.

CLB 4257
© 1995 CLB Publishing

This edition published in 1995 by
SMITHMARK Publishers, Inc.
16 East 32nd Street, New York NY 10016

SMITHMARK books are available for bulk purchase for sales promotion and premium use. For details write or call the manager of special sales, SMITHMARK Publishers, Inc.
16 East 32nd Street, New York,
NY 10016; (212) 532-6600

Produced by CLB Publishing
Godalming Business Centre
Woolsack Way, Godalming, Surrey, UK

ISBN 0-8317-5197-5

Printed in Singapore
10 9 8 7 6 5 4 3 2 1

CONTENTS

INTRODUCTION

Because of their wide geographical distribution, the Jewish people have an incredibly varied and flexible cooking style. Traditional recipes can be traced back to ancient communities, while in North America and Western Europe, new dishes are constantly being introduced by recent immigrants. Add to this the changes caused by contemporary tastes and fashions, and you have an exciting and dynamic style of cooking and eating. Yet, despite its diversity of influences and its modernizations, Jewish cookery retains a recognizable style because it is based on the Jewish dietary laws, and on dishes that celebrate the festivals of the Jewish year.

The interaction among Jewish communities has had a significant effect on diet. For instance, Jews are the only people in the Arab world to eat desserts and cakes at the end of a meal. This European fashion was introduced from Spain by the wealthy, influential Jews who came to Egypt during the Mameluke period of the Middle Ages. The local Jewish population admired the sophisticated lifestyles of these immigrants, and adopted them as well. Similarly, there are many signs of Spanish and Middle Eastern influences in the Jewish foods of Eastern Europe. Such exotic delicacies as citrus fruits, sesame seeds, almonds, olives, olive oil, and rosewater were introduced into the Baltic States, Russia, and Poland by Jewish merchants and travelers from the east. Many of these travelers, such as Benjamin of Tudela and Eldad Hadani, wrote accounts of their journeys.

Jewish cooking in northern Italy has been strongly influenced by Austro-Hungarian cooks. Before World War II, goose was as much a staple of the Jewish diet in Mantua as it was in Cracow, since both cities are located at the extremities of what was once the Austro-Hungarian Empire.

The establishment of the State of Israel is also responsible for a significant change in eating habits. Israel's diverse and prolific agriculture provides a wide variety of produce for the tables of the world, as well as plenty of kosher processed foods. Although Israeli fruits and vegetables are not imported into the western United States, they have influenced Jewish eating habits even there.

Strong influences from outside the Jewish world radically changed the cooking of the Jews. Imports from the New World, such as tomatoes, bell peppers, and chili peppers, are now typical of Sephardic Jewish food, for example. However, the influences have not been all in one direction. The slow-cooking stews prepared for the Sabbath have penetrated other cultures. The Spanish *cocida* and the French *cassoulet* are both of Jewish origin, introduced by the Conversos—Jews forced to convert to Christianity during the Inquisition. Records of this period show that the cooking of such stews was considered a sign of secret adherence to the Jewish faith.

Modern methods of food preparation have had a radical effect on Jewish cooking. Just as the back-breaking work of the kitchen was being abandoned by the modern, working woman, along came appliances that transformed such time-consuming tasks as grinding meat and fish and pureeing vegetables. In fact, the food processor is superior to the hand grinder because it retains the meat and fish juices, and the resulting puree is far tastier.

Even the microwave oven can be used to reproduce many dishes by non-traditional means, cooking in minutes what used to take hours. When a hot meal is required quickly, such as after the Sabbath on Saturday evening and to break the fast on the Day of Atonement, the microwave oven proves invaluable. However, I do not recommend the microwave oven for cooking meat unless it merely has to be reheated.

Early Jewish cookbooks, written in the nineteenth century, were intended to remind newly emancipated Jews of their heritage, which was in danger of being forgotten. Modern Jewish cookbooks should be doing the same thing, though sadly many do not. It is one thing to introduce a dish borrowed from the non-Jewish population if it is commonly eaten in Jewish homes; it is quite another to introduce fancy, *haute cuisine* dishes into a Jewish cookbook just because none of the ingredients violates the dietary laws. It lends such a book a spurious ethnicity, and, in any case, a cook who wanted to try such dishes could find them easily in other cookbooks.

All the recipes in this book are authentic and traditional, with the exception of one curiosity, the Juditha, a recipe invented by, or for, Lady Judith Montefiore, author of the first English-language Jewish cookbook. I have collected these dishes from many sources, in the various countries in which I have lived. My background has been of great help; I am half-Sephardic, half-Ashkenazic. Most of the foods we ate at home were Anglo-Jewish, a combination of such local dishes as roast beef with Yorkshire pudding, *matzo kleis*, and fried fish. But as a concession to my Ashkenazic father, the fried fish was always served with *chrein*.

My father's mother, Bessie Hackman, was a wonderful cook. At her house, my brother and I ate the best chicken soup, boiled chicken, stuffed neck, and wine biscuits. My other grandmother, Dora Jacobs, was a terrible cook, but even though she couldn't boil an egg, her fried fish was absolutely delicious!

Most of my experience with other Jewish communities comes from my ten-year stay in Israel. The man I married, Israeli artist Yehuda Bacon, was born in Czechoslovakia, and his family are all Czech, Slovak, Hungarian, and Polish. We did a lot of entertaining. I learned to cook the dishes he liked and enjoyed the kind of food his sister, Rivka Nedivi, prepared. Before marriage, I had lived on Kibbutz Yotvata, where I often helped in the kitchen. I also visited many other kibbutzim, and experienced what is served in the communal dining rooms.

After leaving Israel, I lived in Cyprus for two years, where I started writing about food, explaining to the wives of British servicemen how to use the exotic, local ingredients such as yogurt and coriander leaves. When I came to live in America, I found that the cooking of American Jews had been strongly influenced by local foods and methods. There were many foods, such as pastrami and knishes, that had been introduced by Jewish immigrants yet were virtually unknown outside the United States. I met many recent immigrants, chiefly from Iran, who were just beginning to play their part in altering the American-Jewish diet.

The first American Jewish cookbook appeared in 1871. *The Jewish Cookery Book* was published in Philadelphia and written by Mrs. Esther Levy née Jacobs. As in *The Jewish Manual*, its predecessor in England, the recipes in Mrs. Levy's book were a mixture of German-Jewish dishes, Sephardic recipes, and Jewish adaptations of Philadelphia regional cooking. American Jewish cookbooks written after the mass immigration of the 1890s and 1900s tended to reproduce the heavier traditional foods and cooking methods of Eastern Europe. Yet our great-grandparents started to change their dietary habits almost as soon as they landed on these shores. The greasy, starchy foods eaten in Central and Eastern Europe—suitable for people living in unheated homes during cold winters and doing heavy manual labor all day—were no longer appropriate. Today's lifestyles stop us from eating these cholesterol-rich foods except on special occasions. Happily, there is no lack of healthful, nourishing everyday foods and festival fare in the modern Jewish diet.

When I taught Jewish cookery in California, I found that my students had the idea that all Jewish food was heavy, indigestible, and tasteless. I sincerely hope this collection of my favorite Jewish recipes will help dispel that notion. The recipes have, in some cases, been adapted to suit current needs and eating habits. For instance, the goose played a crucial part in the Jewish diet of Eastern Europe, but in the United States goose has become unpopular because it is expensive, difficult to cook, hard to carve, and produces so much fat. In most instances, I have replaced the goose in a dish with the native turkey.

My students were interested in finding out what foods they should serve during festivals. I have indicated in the recipe introductions which dishes are appropriate for which festivals. However, I have tried to avoid labeling certain dishes as suitable only for particular occasions, and this includes Passover. I think it is misleading to imply that some dishes are confined to certain events when in reality they can be eaten at any time.

All recipes are marked with symbols indicating whether they are dairy, meat, *pareve* (neither dairy nor meat), and kosher for Passover. An explanation of these terms can be found in the following chapter.

In this book, I have used the terms Ashkenazic, Sephardic, Italian Jewish, Middle Eastern, North African, Yemenite, and Indian; these require some explanation. The divisions into these distinct communities, with their own languages such as Yiddish and Judezmo, have broken down since the Holocaust and the persecution of Jews in the Middle East following the establishment of the State of Israel. By the time this book is published, there will be virtually no Jews left in Iran, for instance. Emigrant Jews have set up their own synagogues and communal institutions in the United States, however, and it is to be hoped that the differences in customs that mark these divisions will not be lost completely.

Ashkenazic is derived from the word *Ashkenaz*, which is found in the Bible and is generally believed to refer to eastern France and Germany. The word is applied to Jews who have been long established in the Pale of Settlement (western Russia and modern Poland), Germany, and most of what was once the Austro-Hungarian Empire.

Sephardic is often used (especially in modern Israel) in a very general way to cover all other Jewish communities. In fact, this is not correct. *Sefarad* is the Biblical name for a country and is now used to refer to Spain. Sephardic Jews are those who lived in Spain and Portugal before the Expulsions and the Inquisitions, which began in the late fifteenth century. Despite being scattered all across the Ottoman Empire, and even reaching Germany and Poland, these Jews still have a strong separate identity. Five hundred years after expulsion, they still speak their own form of Spanish (Judezmo, Ladino, Judeo-Espaniol, or Spaniol), and have very distinctive food styles.

Italian Jewish refers to a community that dates back at least to Roman times and possibly earlier. It is the smallest Jewish community, and lives mostly in Italy and part of Yugoslavia.

Middle Eastern refers to Jewish communities that are as old as the Diaspora itself. The most ancient are the Babylonian Jews from Iraq, who trace their origins to the Babylonian Exile—

believed to have occurred around 800 B.C.E. Jewish communities in Iran, Syria, and the Asian parts of what is now the U.S.S.R. fall into the category of Middle Eastern, as do many Egyptian Jews.

North African refers to Algeria, Morocco, Tunisia, and Libya, since these communities have a history very different from that of Egyptian Jewry. Many Berber tribes converted to Judiasm in the past, and this has had an influence on Jewish cookery in the region. However, there is also a large Sephardic community in North Africa.

Yemenite refers to the Jews from Yemen. Before Mohammed conquered the Arabian Peninsula, there was a Jewish kingdom in the Yemen, at the southern tip of the Arabian Peninsula. The Yemenite Jews were defeated by the followers of Islam and were isolated from the rest of the Jewish world for more than a thousand years, though they remained loyal to the faith throughout this time. However, in the early part of this century, word reached them that a new Jewish home was being set up in Palestine. A few made the journey on foot; almost all the rest were airlifted to Israel in 1949 during "Operation Magic Carpet." Their long period of isolation preserved many unique and fascinating customs in this ancient Jewish community.

Indian Jews refers to one of two separate communities in India: the Beni Israel, who look typically Indian and whose women wear saris; and the Jews of Cochin, whose recipe for Aloo Makalla is included in this book (page 114). (A third large Jewish community in India is the Iraqi community who live in Bombay.)

I hope you enjoy this selection of Jewish recipes, familiar and unfamiliar, and that they will encourage you to introduce them into your regular repertoire of dishes.

1

THE JEWISH DIETARY LAWS

These laws may appear complicated at first glance, but they follow a certain logic. They are based on Divine Law, and there is no question that some of the dietary rules contained in the commandments Moses received on Sinai were amazingly enlightened. Others may seem obscure today, but they probably had their basis in a determination to separate the practices of the monotheists from those of their idol-worshiping neighbors.

KASHRUT AND KOSHER   The concept of what foods are clean or unclean is called *kashrut*, from the Hebrew word *kosher* or *kasher* (depending on which pronunciation is used), meaning "fit" or "proper." Almost all the strictures relating to food concern meat and fish and their by-products; there are no limitations on the consumption of fruits (except in the form of wine) and vegetables.

Most people know that Jews may not eat pork or any product of the pig. There are many more animals and birds that are forbidden; a full list is given in the Bible (Leviticus XI). The Talmud and commentaries thereon have elaborated on these prohibitions and discuss problem cases. Basically, only animals that both chew the cud and have a cloven hoof may be eaten. No birds of prey are kosher, nor are insects, reptiles, or any crawling thing. Yemenite Jews, however, have a tradition of eating locusts, and where such a tradition is established, the rabbis say that it is allowed.

MEAT AND POULTRY   For meat and poultry to be kosher, they must be slaughtered in the traditional way by a qualified *shochet*, a specially trained ritual slaughterer. A knife is used to sever all at once the jugular vein, trachea, esophagus, and the two vagus nerves. The knife must be razor-sharp and completely smooth. This form of slaughter is said to cause the least pain and suffering to the animal while allowing as much blood as possible to drain away.

There is a strong Biblical prohibition on drinking the blood of animals (Leviticus XVII), so as much blood as possible is removed before cooking. When meat and poultry are prepared for cooking, they are first rinsed in lukewarm water to remove all visible blood, then they are soaked in water for thirty minutes, rinsed again, and sprinkled with coarse salt (which for this reason is often known as "kosher salt"). The salt cannot be sprinkled too thickly, since blood must be able to drain through it. The salted meat is drained for one hour on a perforated, slanting board used especially for the purpose. The meat is rinsed again three times and drained. This process is called "koshering." Naturally, ground meat would not come out of this procedure very well, which is why it is bought from a kosher butcher who koshers it before grinding. In fact, most kosher meat bought in the United States is koshered by the butcher before sale.

Heart, such as chicken hearts, must be drained of blood before koshering. The tip of the heart is cut off (though it may be eaten). The heart is then cut open with vertical and horizontal cuts, and washed thoroughly before being koshered with salt and subsequent soaking. Liver is treated slightly differently. It is so full of blood that the only way it can be koshered is to rinse it in cold water, then sprinkle it with salt and sear it (quickly brown the outside) over a naked flame—such as a gas broiler— with a grill underneath to allow the blood to drip through. It can then be prepared in other ways.

Meat must be koshered within seventy-two hours of slaughter, though it may then be frozen or similarly preserved and eaten at a later date. Meat and poultry must not be deep frozen until they have been koshered.

Certain parts of the animal are not kosher, and cannot be eaten by Jews. For example, hindquarter meat is not kosher unless the veins and sinews are removed by a process known as "porging." This custom is a reminder of the injury to Jacob's sinew in his fight with the angel. Since even in Israel porged hindquarter meat is rarely available, no recipes using hindquarter meat are included in this book.

FISH AND SHELLFISH Fish are extremely important in the Jewish diet as a pareve protein source. But not all fish are kosher; fish without fins and scales are strictly prohibited. This includes all shellfish and crustaceans, eels, and fish considered not to have true scales, such as catfish, monkfish, shark, European turbot, and—unfortunately—sturgeon. The kashrus commissions (page 15) keep lists of permitted fish. These lists include all members of the cod family and the trout family (including salmon and whitefish), anchovies, barracuda, bonito, mackerel, mahimahi, mullet, pompano, snappers, and yellowtail. Despite the fact that fish have blood, no special koshering process is needed, so they are quick and easy to prepare.

THE SEPARATION OF MEAT AND DAIRY The lists of forbidden animals are given twice in the Bible, but there is another, even sterner, prohibition repeated three times: "Thou shalt not cook a kid in its mother's milk." This injunction is interpreted to mean that there must be strict separation between milk or milk products and meat or meat products. Milk and meat are never combined in one dish. They are not even eaten at the same meal, and are strictly segregated at every level of preparation. Orthodox Jews who observe the dietary laws keep separate dish-washing bowls, dishwasher racks (or even separate dishwashers!), dishcloths, dishracks, and silverware for meat and milk dishes. Meat and milk dishes are kept on separate shelves of the refrigerator.

It is customary in Jewish communities to wait for up to six hours after eating meat before eating dishes that contain milk (the waiting time varies from one community to another; it can be as short as one hour). After eating milk dishes, one only has to wait thirty minutes before eating meat. The terms *milk, milchig,* or *diary* are commonly used by Jews to describe dishes containing milk and milk products, such as butter, cheese, yogurt, and so on. I have used both *milk* and *dairy* in this book. The terms *meat* or *fleishig* are used to denote meat or poultry dishes.

PAREVE The term *pareve*, pronounced PAR-*veh*, is used to denote foods that do not fall into either the milk or the meat category. All fruits and vegetables are pareve, as well as fish and eggs. Fertilized eggs, however, are unkosher. Jewish housewives are advised to break each egg into a bowl before use and examine it for bloodspots. If any are found, the egg must be discarded.

The origin of the word *pareve* is unknown, however it was once suggested in the British newspaper *The Jewish Chronicle* that it derives from the French word *pauvre*, meaning "poor," because pareve foods are eaten by people too poor to afford kosher meat! The great advantage of pareve is that it can be eaten with either milk or meat dishes. Fortunately, the rabbis have decided that tableware made of glass, because it is nonporous, can be used for milk or meat (however, this does not apply to glass dishes used in the oven).

WINES AND OTHER LIQUORS
Orthodox Jews refuse to drink any wine not labeled kosher. However, wine and liquors containing wine (such as grape brandy) are the only alcohols that must be kosher; grain alcohol may be drunk without restriction. Jews are not forbidden to drink alcohol, and wine is drunk as part of the ritual on every religious occasion—the Sabbath, festivals, weddings, bar mitzvahs, and so on. To be kosher, the grapes must be harvested and the winemaking process completed under supervision. Traditionally, most kosher wines were heavy and sweet, but nowadays there are many excellent kosher dry wines, both domestic and imported.

CHEESES AND GELATIN
Rennet, the substance that curdles milk to produce cheese, is generally produced from the stomach of a ruminant (usually a cow), and therefore renders the cheese nonkosher. Gelatin is produced by boiling down animal bones. Since there are perfectly good vegetable substitutes for both rennet and gelatin, Jews eat only vegetarian cheeses and gelatin.

RESTRICTIONS ON COOKING Cooking is strictly forbidden on the Sabbath. It is usually forbidden during festivals as well, however if the festival day immediately precedes the Sabbath, a special dispensation is allowed, providing the festival is not the Day of Atonement. The dispensation is called an *Eruv Tavshillin*, which means the "mixture of dishes." During the afternoon preceding the festival, a special prayer is recited over two foods—one baked and one boiled. The foods are put aside and eaten during the Sabbath. This preparation for the Sabbath, performed before the festival begins, allows the cook to continue food preparation on the day of the festival itself.

KOSHER FOR PASSOVER Passover foods must be absolutely devoid of leaven. Leaven, as the rabbis understood it, meant anything made with yeast or a food likely to ferment easily, especially flour. During the eight days of Passover, flour is strictly forbidden and is replaced with matzo meal or potato starch. Beer is also strictly forbidden, though wine and distilled liquors are allowed. (Four ritual glasses of wine are drunk during the Passover Seder; for more information on the Passover Seder, see the following section.)

The rabbis did not agree with each other on what other foods could easily ferment, consequently Sephardic and Middle Eastern Jews may eat rice during Passover; Ashkenazic Jews may not.

To avoid the least trace of leaven lingering on dishes and utensils used for Passover, cooks switch to completely separate sets of all kitchenware, tableware, and flatware for both meat and milk dishes. Many Orthodox Jews limit their use of household items such as cleansing powders and even toothpaste to those marked "kosher for Passover."

THE PASSOVER SEDER TABLE   The setting of the Passover table is different from all other meals. The table should be covered with a good cloth. Beside the chair of the person conducting the Seder—preferably on a side table or stand—there should be a pitcher, basin, and towels for the ritual washing of hands. All the chairs should have cushions to enable the diners to "lean" while dining.

In front of the person conducting the Seder there should be a cloth folded or stitched into three compartments for the three ritual pieces of matzo. These matzos should be whole and unbroken. The Passover dish is placed to the right of the cloth and contains the following: a roasted egg, a roasted lamb shank bone, horseradish root and some chervil or lettuce (bitter herbs), a small bowl of salted water, and a bowl of charoset (see page 182).

There should be an extra place set at the table for the symbolic stranger who passes by and is invited in. An extra glass is placed on the table for the prophet Elijah, and it is filled with wine. Each person drinks four glasses of wine, though the children can be given a very small glass or some grape juice.

Passover customs differ from community to community. Among many Ashkenazim, for instance, the first course of the meal is always a hard-cooked egg dipped in salted water. In Iran, green onions (scallions) are on the table and at one point in the service the guests "whip" each other with the onions to symbolize the beatings Hebrew slaves received from their Egyptian masters.

RECIPE CATEGORIES   The following are the terms used in this book to denote the categories of foods. These categories will help you combine various foods to build interesting menus.

- meat
- dairy
- pareve
- kosher for Passover
- can be slow-cooked for the Sabbath

It is assumed throughout the book that meat has been koshered in the prescribed manner, therefore the procedures for koshering have been omitted from the recipes. It is also assumed that all eggs are large unless specified, and that all flour is presifted. All spoon and cup measures are level, and all fruits and vegetables are medium unless indicated. Where margarine is mentioned, the reference is to kosher pareve margarine (without milk or animal fat). Where shortening is listed, use pareve shortening or chicken fat substitute.

If you would like more information on Jewish dietary laws, apply to the Jewish religious authorities responsible for the supervision of kosher meat and other kosher foods in your locality.

Kashrut Division
Union of Orthodox Hebrew
Congregations of America
84 Fifth Avenue
New York, New York 10001
U.S.A.

Sydney and N.S.W. Kashrus Commission
140 Darlinghurst Road
Darlinghurst, New South Wales 2010
AUSTRALIA

Beth Din
5491 Victoria Avenue 26
Quebec
CANADA

Joint Kashrus Commission
Union of Orthodox Hebrew
Congregations
Queen Elizabeth Walk
London N 16
ENGLAND

Belfast Shechita Board
Somerton Road Synagogue
Somerton Road
Belfast
NORTHERN IRELAND

General Board of Shechita of Eire
Zion Schools
Bloomfield Road
Dublin 8
IRELAND

Edinburgh Shechita Board
Synagogue
4 Salisbury Road
Edinburgh
SCOTLAND

Cardiff Board of Shechita
The Synagogue
Cathedral Road
Cardiff
WALES

2
APPETIZERS AND SNACKS

Appetizers are very important in Jewish cookery, though they have been borrowed from the traditions of the countries in which the largest Jewish communities have settled. There is the Russian tradition of *zakuski*, the wide variety of tidbits that always includes smoked fish and which precedes any important meal. In the Middle East there is the *mezze*, a word derived from the Latin *mensa*, meaning "table"; in Lebanon, a Jewish hostess would have been ashamed to serve a *mezze* of less than thirty dishes!

These vast assortments were the appetizers that appeared on the tables of the rich. But until very recently the large majority of Jews were working class and poor, and appetizers were used to take the edge off the appetite when the main dish was not plentiful. Today appetizers represent the taste of delicious things to come.

Tarator

This appetizer, also known as *cacık* (pronounced *CHA-chik*), is popular in the Sephardic communities of the Balkans. It is extremely simple to make, and is delicious in summer when cucumbers are in season. Try to use extra-virgin olive oil, which usually has a greenish color and is more flavorful.

dairy, kosher for Passover

SERVES 8

4 short or 2 long cucumbers
1 clove garlic
½ teaspoon coarse salt
2 cups plain yogurt

½ teaspoon olive oil
1 teaspoon lemon juice
1 tablespoon chopped fresh dill

Peel the cucumbers and cut them into small dice. Crush the garlic clove with the salt, and stir it into the yogurt. Add the olive oil and lemon juice and mix well.

Put the cucumber into a salad bowl and add the yogurt mixture. Stir well. Sprinkle with dill before serving. Serve with pita bread, warmed and cut into quarters.

Kibbutz Carrot Salad

This is an Israeli invention, which I first tasted (and learned to make) on Kibbutz Yotvata, at the southern end of Israel near the Timnah copper mines. In Israel the carrots are so sweet they need no sweetener, but use the sugar here sparingly.

pareve, kosher for Passover

SERVES 6

2½ pounds young carrots
juice of 3 large oranges
juice of 2 lemons
1 cup water

1 tablespoon brown sugar or clear honey
orange or lemon slices
raisins or mint leaves

Grate the carrots into a large bowl. Strain the orange and lemon juices and pour over. Add water and the brown sugar or honey. Stir well.

Cover the bowl with plastic wrap and refrigerate for at least 2 hours to allow the flavors to mingle. To serve, decorate with orange and lemon slices, or a few raisins or mint leaves.

Tahina

This sesame-seed paste can be bought ready-made from Greek and Middle Eastern grocery stores. If you have a blender or food processor, however, it is easy to make at home. Tahina is eaten as a dip with raw vegetables, such as peeled cucumbers, cherry tomatoes, bell pepper slices, lettuce leaves, and green onions (scallions).

pareve

MAKES 1½ CUPS

1¼ cups sesame seeds
1 cup water
2 cloves garlic

juice of 2 lemons
½ teaspoon salt

Place all the ingredients in a blender or food processor. Blend on high until you have a thick, smooth paste. If tahina is not to be used immediately, store it in a closed jar in the refrigerator, where it will keep for several months. The sesame oil tends to separate out of the paste, so stir again before using.

Herrings with Apple-Roe Puree

Fresh Baltic herrings are unobtainable in the United States, as indeed they were in landlocked prewar Poland, Hungary, and Czechoslovakia. Herrings were salted and sent in barrels from the Danzig (Gdansk) and other Baltic ports. North Sea herrings also arrived from the Netherlands. Herrings were a cheap source of protein, and became a staple of the Jewish diet.

Salted, pickled, and cured herrings are available in bulk at Jewish delis and can also be found in jars at the supermarket. They make a delicious appetizer, served with Jewish rye or black bread. Here is a classic Polish recipe for salt herrings.

pareve, kosher for Passover

SERVES 4

4 salt herrings, with soft roe, soaked in
   water for 3 hours
2 large green apples, peeled and cored
2 onions, quartered

4 tablespoons ground almonds
2 tablespoons oil
2 pickles, sliced

Drain the herrings and rinse them again in fresh water. Remove the roe from the fish and reserve. Cut the herrings into ½-inch slices. Put the apples, onions, and almonds into a blender or food processor and grind until the mixture is smooth. Add the roe and the oil and grind again.

Have ready 4 small dishes. Spread the pureed roe mixture evenly on each dish and arrange the sliced herrings on top. Serve with pickles and black bread.

Herring Spread with Sour Cream

These herrings can be made with yogurt instead of sour cream if you want a lower-calorie version. Fresh herbs, such as parsley, chervil, or coriander, can also be added to the mixture.

dairy, kosher for Passover

SERVES 8

4 herrings, preferably with hard roe, soaked in water for 3 hours
2 cups sour cream

2 tablespoons mayonnaise
1 potato, boiled and peeled
½ teaspoon black pepper

Drain the herrings and rinse with water. Fillet the fish, removing all bones.

In a bowl, blend the roe with the sour cream and mayonnaise. Puree the potato in a food processor or blender and add the herrings. Blend well, then stir the herring mixture into the sour-cream mixture and season with pepper. Chill, covered, until ready to use, then serve as a spread for crackers or matzo.

✡

Cocktail Fish Balls

This is an adaptation of the basic Gefilte Fish recipe (page 72). It is popular with Ashkenazic Jews, especially those in Britain and the United States, who serve it on any festive occasion. Use a single kind of fish or a mixture of types. Almost any fish is suitable, but fatty fish (tuna, mackerel, bonito, herring) should only be used in combination with a lean fish (porgy, red snapper, etc.).

pareve

SERVES 6

3 pounds fish, cleaned but not filleted
3 eggs, 2 separated and 1 lightly beaten
4 slices white bread, crusts removed,
   soaked in water, and squeezed dry
½ teaspoon salt
½ teaspoon paprika
½ teaspoon black pepper
1 cup fine matzo meal
oil for deep-frying

COURT-BOUILLON
1 large onion, sliced
1 carrot, split lengthwise
1 leek, sliced
8 sprigs fresh parsley
1 teaspoon dried thyme
2 teaspoons fresh dill
1 bay leaf
1 cup white wine vinegar
6 black peppercorns
1 quart water

Put the court-bouillon ingredients into a pot. Add water and bring to a boil on high heat. Cover and cook for 10 minutes. Add the fish, and reduce the heat to minimum; the water should barely move. Partially cover the pot and simmer for 30 minutes.

Remove the fish from the pot. Discard the skin and bones, and flake the flesh. Place the flesh in a food processor with the egg yolks, soaked bread, salt, paprika, and pepper. Puree until smooth. Whip the egg whites until they form stiff peaks, then fold them into the fish mixture.

Pour the matzo meal into a shallow dish, and place the beaten egg in another. Wet your hands and roll the fish mixture into balls about the size of a walnut. Dip the balls first in the egg, then in the matzo meal. Place enough oil in a deep-fryer to come 2 inches up the sides of the fryer. Heat until temperature reaches 365°F. If you have a fryer basket, put about 6 fish balls into the basket and lower basket into the hot oil. If not using a basket, lower the fish balls into the oil with a skimmer. Fry quickly, turning if necessary. Drain the cooked fish balls on absorbent paper. Repeat until all fish balls have been cooked. Serve cold, on cocktail sticks.

PASSOVER VARIATION
Replace the bread with 2 pieces matzo.

NOTE
Don't waste the court-bouillon. What's left can be strained, then frozen and used later as a fish broth, fish soup, or poaching liquid for more fish.

Chopped Liver

Here is another typically Ashkenazic dish. There are really 2 versions, the coarsely chopped, which is my favorite, and the smooth liver pâté type, which is more elegant. This first version is the coarser.

meat, kosher for Passover

SERVES 8

6 tablespoons chicken fat
4 large white or yellow onions, coarsely
   chopped

1 pound koshered chicken livers
½ teaspoon black pepper
½ teaspoon salt

Melt the fat in a large skillet and sauté the onions until golden. Remove from the skillet. Sauté the chicken livers briefly in the same pan just long enough to warm them and coat them with fat. Remove livers from pan and combine with onions, chopping together. Season well with pepper and salt. Serve with rye bread or matzo.

Chicken Liver Pâté

Here is a smooth pâté, ideal for a cocktail party. The eggs help dilute the flavor of the livers, which some people find too strong.

meat, kosher for Passover

SERVES 12 TO 15

6 tablespoons chicken fat
2 pounds koshered chicken livers
3 large white or yellow onions, cut in
   quarters

4 hard-cooked eggs, halved
½ teaspoon salt
½ teaspoon pepper

Melt the chicken fat in a large skillet and briefly sauté the chicken livers over high heat until well-browned. Remove livers and place in blender or food processor along with onions, hard-cooked eggs, salt, and pepper. Blend to a smooth paste, then taste for seasoning. Serve with crackers or matzos.

Chopped Calves' Liver

Yet another liver recipe! The sweet-and-sour flavor of this typically Polish appetizer makes it worth trying as a variation on the traditional theme.

meat, kosher for Passover

SERVES 6

4 tablespoons chicken fat	salt and black pepper
8 ounces koshered calves' liver	pinch of sugar
1 white or yellow onion, finely chopped	2 tablespoons cider vinegar

Melt half the chicken fat in a large skillet and briefly sauté the calves' liver over high heat. Cut the liver into bite-sized pieces and place in a food processor or meat grinder. Grind the liver with half the onion. Place mixture in a bowl. Add the salt, pepper, sugar, and vinegar, and, stirring constantly, add the rest of the onion. Serve with black bread or matzo.

Nahit

Nahit, also known as *bob* (Yiddish for "beans"), are chick peas as they are eaten in Russia and Poland. In Poland, it was traditional for Jews to eat these on the birth of a child. Chick peas, and also green peas, are symbols of the continuity of life because they are round. This recipe is also associated with Purim in western Russia and Poland.

pareve

SERVES 6

2 cups chick peas, soaked overnight in water to cover	½ cup clear honey
1 teaspoon salt	½ cup water
1 tablespoon oil	½ teaspoon ground cinnamon

Drain the chick peas. Put them in a saucepan in water to cover and bring to a boil. Boil for 1 hour or until tender. Preheat the oven to 350°F. Drain the chick peas, discarding any remaining cooking liquid, and place in an ovenproof serving dish. Combine the salt, oil, honey, water, and cinnamon. Pour this over the chick peas. Bake for 30 minutes, basting with the liquid after 15 minutes cooking. Serve warm.

Falafel

Falafel is the national dish of both Israel and Egypt, though it is eaten everywhere in the Arab world. It is a coarse paste of chick peas (garbanzo beans), or chick peas and field beans, that is spiced, shaped into small pieces, and deep-fried. Arab falafel is darker-colored and shaped like a tiny patty; Israeli falafel is golden brown and globular.

Falafel is eaten as a snack, packed in pita bread with plenty of lettuce, tomato, and cucumber. It is generally accompanied by a hot sauce containing fenugreek, a bitter herb. A similar sauce can be made by mixing Tabasco or similar pepper sauce with tomato sauce. Bulgur (partially cooked cracked wheat) can be bought at Greek or Middle Eastern stores.

pareve

SERVES 8

1 cup chick peas, soaked overnight in
   water to cover
1 slice white bread, crust removed
2 cloves garlic, minced
2 tablespoons chopped fresh parsley
¼ cup bulgur, rinsed and drained

½ teaspoon ground coriander
½ teaspoon ground cumin
½ teaspoon cayenne pepper
1 teaspoon salt
oil for deep-frying

Drain and rinse the chick peas in fresh water. Grind them in a food processor or blender, putting them through twice if necessary to make a coarse paste.

Soak the bread in water, and squeeze it dry by hand. Chop it with the minced garlic and the parsley. Add this mixture to the chick peas. Add the bulgur, spices, and salt and mix well. Leave in the refrigerator for 30 minutes.

In a deep-fat fryer, preferably with a frying basket, heat the oil to very hot, about 350°F, or until a cube of bread will brown in 60 seconds. Wet your hands and shape the mixture into small balls about the size of a walnut. Deep-fry the balls a few at a time for 2 to 3 minutes or until golden. Remove with a skimmer and transfer to absorbent paper to drain in a warm place. Serve immediately with mixed salad. Falafel are best when eaten very fresh. Do not store.

Falafel and Hummus

Hummus is the Arabic and Hebrew word for chick pea. In Israel, it usually refers to a chick pea paste, popular as an appetizer throughout the Middle East. Homemade hummus is much tastier than the canned and packaged varieties, because you can alter the flavoring to suit your tastes and also reserve a few chick peas for decoration.

pareve

SERVES 6

2 cups chick peas, soaked overnight in
    water to cover
½ teaspoon salt
2 cloves garlic
juice of 2 lemons
8 tablespoons Tahina (recipe page 18)

¼ cup olive oil
1 batch Falafel (recipe page 24)
6 tablespoons chopped fresh parsley
6 hard-cooked eggs
½ teaspoon cayenne pepper

Drain the chick peas and rinse in fresh water. Drain again, and put the chick peas in a saucepan; add salt and fresh water to cover. Bring to a boil and simmer, partially covered, for 1 hour or until tender, adding water if necessary.

Drain the chick peas. Reserve 16 chick peas for a garnish. Blend the garlic, salt, and lemon juice in a food processor or blender. Gradually add the remaining chick peas and blend until smooth. If the mixture appears too dry to puree, add a little water or oil.

Have ready 8 small shallow dishes. Divide the hummus evenly among the dishes, spreading it well over each dish. Drizzle a swirl of tahina about 1 inch from the edge of each plate. Sprinkle the olive oil at the center of each plate, and place 2 whole chick peas in the center.

Cook the falafel and arrange balls neatly round the edge of the dishes. Sprinkle the center of each plate liberally with parsley. Cut the hard-cooked eggs lengthwise into quarters and arrange them on the dishes. Sprinkle the center of the dish and the egg yolks with cayenne pepper. Serve immediately, with pita bread. Use the bread to scoop up the dip.

Bourekas

I once saw a pile of these tasty pastries in the Los Angeles Grand Central Market. I recognized them immediately, especially since the traditional hard-cooked eggs were alongside them. I approached the stall-owner who, seeing my dark complexion, immediately addressed me in Spanish. I pointed to the pastries and asked him in English what they were. "They are a Turkish specialty," he replied.

"No, they aren't," I responded in Hebrew. "They are bourekas!" We both laughed. He was a Turkish Jew who spoke Judezmo, the Spanish of his ancestors who fled from the Inquisition. He was selling these traditional Jewish pastries made by his wife to the local Mexican and Chicano population.

Miniature bourekas are served as cocktail snacks. The dimensions here are for the larger, heartier versions. Phyllo pastry can be bought in supermarkets as well as in Greek and Middle Eastern delis. The sheets of dough come in 1-pound packages. If you use only a few leaves, wrap the remainder well; phyllo dough will keep indefinitely in the freezer.

These quantities assume you are going to make both fillings at one session. If you only make one of the fillings, halve the quantity of dough.

cheese filling: dairy
spinach filling: pareve

MAKES ABOUT 72 LARGE PASTRIES

1 pound phyllo dough, thawed if frozen
about 2 cups butter or margarine (depending on whether filling is milk or pareve), melted
1 cup sesame seeds
1 beaten egg (optional)

CHEESE FILLING
2 cups crumbled feta cheese
2 eggs, lightly beaten
4 tablespoons chopped fresh parsley
½ teaspoon black pepper

SPINACH FILLING
2 cups (1 pound) fresh spinach, or 8 ounces frozen leaf spinach, thawed
1 tablespoon margarine
2 tablespoons lemon juice
¼ teaspoon grated nutmeg
2 tablespoons oil
⅓ cup slivered almonds
1 egg, lightly beaten
salt and pepper

First prepare the fillings. Leave the dough in its package until you are just about to use it. It dries out very quickly when exposed to the air, so as you work with it, keep any unused portions covered with a damp kitchen towel.

To make the cheese filling, crumble the feta with a fork. Add the rest of the ingredients and work the mixture into a paste. Cover and reserve.

To make the spinach filling, trim the spinach stems, then wash and chop the spinach finely. Put it in a saucepan with the margarine, lemon juice, and nutmeg. Cover and cook on low heat until the spinach is wilted—5 minutes for fresh spinach, 2 minutes for defrosted.

Heat the oil in a small skillet and sauté the almonds until lightly browned; drain on absorbent paper. Combine almonds with the spinach, then bind with the beaten egg. Season to taste with salt and pepper.

Preheat the oven to 400°F. Lightly grease a large cookie sheet. Lay a sheet of phyllo dough on another cookie sheet. Brush it with some melted butter for the cheese filling, margarine for the spinach filling. Use a sharp knife to slice the sheet lengthwise into 4 equal-sized strips. Place 1 teaspoon of the filling about 1 inch from the top left-hand corner of each strip. Fold the corner of the dough over the filling, making a triangle, then continue to fold the triangle down over the strip of dough until the whole is a triangular package. Brush with melted butter or beaten egg. Sprinkle with a few sesame seeds and set aside onto prepared cookie sheet. Repeat the procedure until all the dough and fillings are used up. Bake the pastries for 20 minutes, or until golden brown. Serve as quickly as possible.

NOTE

You can make smaller bourekas by cutting each sheet of dough into 6, instead of 4, strips. The smaller the bourekas, the less baking time they will need. Serve larger bourekas with hard-cooked eggs, smaller ones with cocktails.

3

SOUPS

Soup plays a central part in the Jewish diet. It is generally inexpensive, easy to prepare, comforting and nourishing, and when prepared with meat, makes the cheapest cuts taste good. The most important flavoring ingredients in any soup are the vegetables. The best cooks have never seen a stock cube; their flavorings are the root vegetables, leafy vegetables, and fresh herbs without which even the best cuts of meat would leave a soup tasteless. All clear soups freeze well, so strain vegetables and meats beforehand.

Classic Chicken Soup

Chicken soup is a Jewish favorite all over the world. Among East European Jews it had a ritual significance because it was served to a bride and groom to break their wedding-day fast. Jewish chicken soup has become symbolic of Jewish cooking. Amazingly, scientists have discovered that chicken soup really does help cure a cold, so it's not just an old wives' tale!

Try to use larger, older fowls, since they have more flavor. Add the gizzard, neck, and heart to the soup whenever possible. Some Jewish cooks also add the feet (Romanian Jews consider the feet a delicacy!), which are believed to add flavor; just remove them before serving the soup.

With modern poultry rearing, it is rare to find unhatched eggs inside a chicken, but if you do, they make a delicious addition to the soup. For kashrut purposes, unhatched eggs are considered meat, not *pareve* as are hatched eggs, so they must be koshered in the same way as meat.

If the chicken in this recipe is to be eaten separately, you may find it tastier if you brown it first in a little chicken fat.

meat

SERVES 6 TO 8

1 large chicken, about 3 pounds, with giblets	2 large white turnips, quartered
1 large onion, stuck with 2 cloves	1 stalk celery, coarsely chopped
2 carrots, sliced	1 teaspoon salt
1 bunch (about 8 ounces) fresh parsley	¼ teaspoon white pepper

Scald the chicken by pouring boiling water over it inside and out. Put the chicken into a stew pot or Dutch oven. Add water to cover and place pot over high heat. Bring the water to a boil, skimming off the foam as it accumulates. When the water boils, reduce the heat and add the vegetables. Cover the pot and simmer for 3 hours over very low heat.

Remove the chicken from the pot and serve it separately or cut it into serving pieces and add it to soup just before serving. Strain the soup, discarding the vegetables. Wipe the surface with a paper towel to soak up excess fat. Or, better still, cool the soup, refrigerate it, and remove the fat which will have solidified on top; then reheat soup. Taste soup, and add the seasonings before serving.

Israeli Chicken Soup with Pasta

This is a slightly simplied form of a lemon-flavored chicken soup, popular in the North African communities of Israel. The Algerians prefer it mild, while the Tunisians add enough hot red pepper to burn the roof off your mouth. This is the milder version, but you can add more chili pepper to your liking. (Chicken is usually sold in pieces in Israel because so many Israelis do not have baking ovens and cannot roast whole chickens.)

meat

SERVES 6 TO 8

1 large chicken, about 3 pounds, cut in 8 serving pieces	*2 white turnips, quartered*
salt and black pepper	*2 carrots, sliced lengthwise*
1 teaspoon ground cinnamon	*2 quarts water*
4 tablespoons vegetable oil	*½ lemon, seeds removed*
2 onions, sliced	*¼ teaspoon turmeric*
4 tablespoons chopped fresh parsley	*½ teaspoon chili pepper*
4 tablespoons chopped fresh coriander (cilantro)	*2 cups Farfel (recipe page 52)*
	parsley sprigs
	lemon wedges

Season the chicken pieces with salt, pepper, and cinnamon. Heat the oil in a large saucepan or flameproof casserole over medium heat, and sauté the chicken pieces and onions until the chicken flesh is firm and the onions transparent. This will take about 10 minutes.

Add the vegetables and water and bring to a boil. Squeeze the lemon into the liquid, then drop the squeezed lemon half into the soup. Add the turmeric and chili powder and cover pot. Reduce heat and simmer for 1½ hours or until the chicken is tender.

Add the pasta to the soup and simmer another 5 minutes. Serve soup with the chicken pieces, or, alternately, remove the chicken from the pot and serve it separately as a main course. To serve soup, ladle it into warmed, individual bowls and garnish with parsley sprigs. Serve lemon wedges separately so diners can squeeze the lemon into the soup.

Chicken Soup with Ground Almonds

The ground almonds in this Polish recipe show a Sephardic influence. Ground almonds or almond meal can be bought in a specialty store, but you can easily grind 20 blanched almonds in a food processor for the same results.

This is an excellent recipe for cooking overnight on the Sabbath and serving at lunchtime the following day. If you are not making this soup over the Sabbath and have a microwave oven, speed up the cooking by transferring the contents of the stew pot to a suitable pot and microwaving on medium for 30 minutes.

meat
can be slow-cooked for the Sabbath

SERVES 6 TO 8

1 tablespoon chicken fat
3 carrots, julienned
2 leeks (white parts only), thinly sliced
2 tablespoons all-purpose flour
½ teaspoon salt

4 tablespoons ground almonds
1 large chicken, about 3 pounds, cut in
    8 serving pieces
1 quart water
½ teaspoon paprika

Melt the chicken fat in a stew pot or Dutch oven over high heat. Add the vegetables and sauté until they start to color, then stir in the flour and allow it to brown lightly. Add enough warm water to cover the contents of the pan (about 2 cups). Season with the salt and add ground almonds. Cover pot and simmer over low heat for 30 minutes.

Add the chicken pieces to the soup. Add water and the paprika. Cover pot tightly and simmer over very low heat or in an oven at 250°F for at least 3 hours.

Remove and discard the chicken bones. Strain the soup through a sieve and puree the solids in a blender or food processor. Mix the puree with the liquid, season to taste, and reheat. Serve very hot.

Sweet-and-Sour Cabbage Soup

Sweet-and-sour flavors are as prevalent in Eastern European Jewish cooking as they are in Chinese. The caraway seeds are also extremely popular; my former husband, who was from Czechoslovakia, ate them like candy! The sourness is often achieved with citric acid—also called sour salt—which is sold in supermarkets and pharmacies. Use the white crystals sparingly, as they have a very strong flavor.

The technique of pureeing the vegetables and returning them to the soup is very typical of German (non-Jewish) cooking. To peel the tomatoes, immerse them in boiling water for a few minutes, then slip off the skins. Discard the tomato seeds while retaining as much of the juice as possible.

meat, kosher for Passover

SERVES 6 TO 8

1 small head green cabbage, about 1½ pounds	1 teaspoon citric acid crystals
1 pound beef top of rib or shortribs	1 tablespoon Worcestershire sauce (omit for Passover)
2 quarts water	1 tablespoon caraway seeds
½ teaspoon salt	1 onion, stuck with 2 cloves
½ teaspoon black pepper	3 large tomatoes, peeled, seeded, and chopped
3 tablespoons brown sugar	

Shred the cabbage and put into a large soup pot or stew pot. Add the meat and water and bring to a boil over high heat. Skim the surface to remove scum, then reduce the heat, cover the pot, and simmer for 45 minutes.

Add the remaining ingredients to the pot and continue simmering, covered, for 2 hours.

Remove the meat from the pot and strain the soup, discarding the cloves. Skim the surface of the soup with a paper towel to remove excess fat. Bone the meat if you have used shortribs. Discard any fat. Puree the vegetables in a food processor or blender. Add pureed vegetables and meat to soup and reheat before serving. Alternately, you could serve meat separately as the entree.

Beef Soup with Kasha

Kasha—buckwheat groats—is a basic ingredient of the Russian diet. It has a very distinctive flavor, so if you have never tasted it before, use it sparingly. Kasha is easy to find in the kosher section of most supermarkets.

The meat in this Russian soup is expensive, so it is usually served separately as an entree with Dill Pickles (page 177) and Latkes (see page 112). The soup is also very suitable for slow-cooking overnight to serve at lunchtime the following day.

meat, can be slow-cooked for Sabbath

SERVES 6 TO 8

4 pounds beef rib roast, trimmed of fat	2 leeks, trimmed and split lengthwise
3 quarts water	3 onions, quartered
1 teaspoon salt	2 cloves garlic, crushed
3 large carrots, split lengthwise	1 bunch fresh parsley
2 white turnips, quartered	2 cups kasha

Place the meat in a soup pot along with 2 quarts water. Bring to a boil over high heat, skimming the surface to remove scum. When liquid boils, add remaining ingredients including additional quart of water. Cover pot and reduce heat. Simmer soup at just below boiling point for 3 hours.

Remove the meat and cut into serving pieces. Chop the vegetables coarsely. Return meat and vegetables to the pot and reheat. Serve hot.

Sopa de Albóndigas

The most economical meat is chopped or ground, because it can be stretched with extenders such as grain or bread. This meatball soup, which has several names, is popular throughout the Sephardic community; a recipe for it is included in the first English-language Jewish cookbook, *The Jewish Manual*, written in 1842 by "a Lady." Her version did not include the exotic—and potentially dangerous?—vegetable she refers to elsewhere in her book as a "tomata." This is a version I enjoyed in a Sephardic home in Los Angeles.

meat

SERVES 8

1 carrot, diced
1 leek, sliced
1 rutabaga, sliced
1 parsnip, sliced
4 tomatoes, peeled and chopped
2 quarts water or broth
2 tablespoons tomato paste
salt and black pepper

FOR THE MEATBALLS
1½ pounds lean ground beef or lamb
1 cup cooked white rice
2 eggs, lightly beaten
salt and pepper

Place the vegetables in a large soup pot. Add the water or broth and bring to a boil over high heat. Reduce the heat to a simmer and let cook for 30 minutes.

While the soup is cooking, combine the ingredients for the meatballs. Wet your hands and shape the mixture into walnut-sized balls. Drop the balls into the boiling broth, then add the tomato paste. Season to taste with salt and pepper. When the soup returns to a boil, ladle individual servings.

Hot Borscht

This very popular spring-beet soup takes on many forms, most of which fall into 3 basic types: hot with beef and beets, hot but meatless, and cold meatless. This recipe is for a meatless soup enriched with pureed vegetables and thickened slightly with beaten egg. The old-fashioned Russian way of making borscht uses the nutritious young beet leaves. Among East European Jews, the beets were often fermented before the soup was made.

meat, kosher for Passover

SERVES 8

2 pounds beef brisket
2 pounds beef marrow bones
3 quarts water
6 young beets, with tops
1 teaspoon salt
½ teaspoon black pepper

1 bay leaf
2 onions, quartered
1 clove garlic
4 tablespoons brown sugar
½ cup red wine vinegar
2 eggs, lightly beaten

Place the meat and bones in a large soup pot along with the water. Bring to a boil over high heat, skimming the foam. While the water is heating, cut off the beet tops and chop them roughly. Peel and trim the beets, then quarter them.

When water boils, add the beets and tops to the pot along with the seasonings, bay leaf, onions, and garlic. Bring the liquid back to a boil, reduce the heat, cover, and simmer for 2 hours.

Strain the soup. Remove the meat and bones, reserving the meat for your entree and discarding the bones. Discard the bay leaf. Puree the vegetables in a blender or food processor and return them to the soup. Pour the soup back into the pot, but reserve 1 cup of liquid. Stir the sugar and vinegar into the soup.

Beat the eggs into the reserved cup of soup, and pour this mixture back into the soup. Heat the soup to just below boiling, stirring constantly to prevent curdling, and serve hot.

Lentil Soup

No Jewish cookbook would be complete without the soup for which Esau sold his birthright. You can use water instead of beef broth, and vegetable shortening instead of chicken fat, in which case the soup becomes pareve. This version is very popular in Israel in the winter. It is another soup that can be simmered in a very slow oven overnight, once the fried onion has been added.

meat, can be slow-cooked for Sabbath

SERVES 8

2 quarts beef broth or consommé	2 onions, 1 stuck with 2 cloves
2 cups red or brown lentils, rinsed, soaked overnight, and drained	2 stalks celery, roughly chopped
	1 bay leaf
1 carrot, coarsely chopped	2 tablespoons chicken fat

Pour the broth or consommé into a soup pot and add the lentils, carrot, onion stuck with cloves, celery, and bay leaf. Bring to a boil over high heat. Reduce the heat, cover, and simmer for 30 minutes.

Slice the remaining onion. Melt the fat in a skillet and sauté the onion over medium heat until it just begins to color. Transfer it to the soup.

Continue to simmer soup, stirring occasionally, for 90 minutes. Dip a cup into the soup and remove some soup and lentils. Puree the cup of soup in a blender or food processor, and return it to the soup, to thicken the liquid. (More lentils can be pureed if a thicker consistency is preferred.)

Bean Soup

There are many versions of this soup, most of them Sephardic, and they originate from places as far apart as Holland and Greece. This particular version is standard winter fare in Israel, where it is served in every restaurant.

In Israel, brown or field beans (called *ful*) are used, as these are native to the Middle East. Suitable substitutes are navy beans, white great northern beans, and lima beans. Never add salt to beans before they are soft; it toughens the skins.

pareve

SERVES 8

2 cups dried beans, soaked overnight in
   water to cover
2 quarts water
1 bay leaf
6 black peppercorns
1 tablespoon margarine

1 large onion, thinly sliced
1 teaspoon chili pepper
1 tablespoon tomato paste
salt
4 tablespoons chopped fresh parsley

Drain the beans, discarding the water. Put them in a soup pot and add water. Bring to a boil over high heat, then reduce the heat and add the bay leaf and peppercorns. Cover and cook over low heat for 30 to 45 minutes, or until the beans are soft.

While the soup is cooking, melt the margarine in a skillet and sauté the onion over medium heat until it is transparent but not browned. Add onion to the cooked beans along with the chili pepper and tomato paste. Cover and simmer for 15 minutes.

Add salt to taste, and more pepper if desired. To serve, discard the bay leaf, pour the soup into individual bowls, and sprinkle with parsley.

Krupnik

Krupnik is mushroom-barley soup. Wild mushrooms are available from gourmet food stores and sometimes supermarkets. Use boletes (*cepes* or *porcini*), but avoid Chinese or Japanese dried mushrooms. If you cannot find dried mushrooms, you could substitute fresh button mushrooms, but the flavor will be considerably diminished.

pareve

SERVES 8 TO 10

1 cup pearl barley
3 quarts water
3 carrots
3 white turnips, peeled

1 yellow turnip, peeled and halved
½ cup dried mushrooms
1 teaspoon salt
½ teaspoon black pepper

Put the barley in a soup pot along with the water. Add the root vegetables, cover the pot, and bring to a boil over high heat. Reduce the heat, cover, and simmer just below boiling point for 3 hours.

Remove 1 cup of the soup. Soak the mushrooms in this liquid for 20 minutes, then drain.

If the mushroom soaking liquid becomes gritty, strain it through cheesecloth, then add it and the mushrooms to the soup. Simmer for an additional 15 minutes before serving.

Romanian Tomato Soup

At last, a quick soup! Romania is one of the few countries with indigenous Sephardic and Ashkenazic communities, so there is a strong mutual influence in the cooking. I first ate this soup at the house of some inlaws. Although the wife is from the Ashkenazic Romanian community, this soup is typically Sephardic.

Use meat broth instead of water if you are making this for a meat meal. A handful of herbs such as basil or oregano can be added, though this is not traditional.

pareve

SERVES 8

3 quarts water
1 cup uncooked long-grain rice
½ teaspoon salt
3 pounds tomatoes, peeled, seeded, and
  coarsely chopped

1 tablespoon sugar
¼ teaspoon paprika

Place water in a soup pot and add the rice and salt. Bring to a boil over high heat, then reduce heat, cover, and cook 10 minutes. Add the tomatoes and sugar to the pot. Simmer for 15 minutes more, or until rice is soft. Add paprika and taste for seasoning, adding more sugar if necessary.

✡

Cold Borscht

This is another Israeli favorite, and very refreshing in the hot summers of the Middle East. It is one of the few clear soups, although sometimes a few shreds of grated beet are sprinkled on top for decoration.

Cold borscht is usually served in a glass. Some people like it clear and a deep ruby red; others prefer a thicker consistency, achieved by beating in a cup of plain yogurt or sour cream just before serving. If serving this way, decorate the soup with thinly sliced cucumber and offer more yogurt or sour cream on the side.

pareve; with yogurt or sour cream: dairy

SERVES 6

6 cups water
2 large or 3 small cooked and peeled
  beets, finely chopped
1 teaspoon salt

2 tablespoons lemon juice
2 tablespoons sugar
plain yogurt or sour cream (optional)

Place water in a soup pot and bring to a boil over high heat. Add the beets. Cover the pot and bring the water back to a boil. Reduce the heat and simmer for 10 minutes. Add the salt, lemon juice, and sugar, and cook 5 minutes. Strain the soup and chill thoroughly before serving.

Shchav

This Russian soup is made with sorrel (also called sour grass). However, since sorrel is hard to find unless you grow it yourself, substitute young spinach leaves or even Swiss chard leaves (ribs discarded). Shchav is often eaten on Shavuot, the Feast of Weeks.

dairy, kosher for Passover

SERVES 8

2 quarts vegetable broth
1 bunch watercress, chopped
1 pound sorrel or spinach, washed well
  and coarsely chopped
1 stalk celery, finely chopped

juice and grated rind of 1 lemon
3 tablespoons sugar
½ teaspoon salt
½ teaspoon white pepper
2 cups sour cream

Place the broth in a soup pot and add the watercress, sorrel or spinach, and celery. Bring to a boil over high heat, then simmer for 45 minutes.

If you have used spinach, the leaves may not have completely dissolved in the liquid. If so, cool the soup, then puree it in a blender or food processor. Return soup to the pot, and reheat.

Add the lemon juice and grated rind, sugar, salt, and white pepper. Transfer soup to a nonmetal container and cover with plastic wrap. Refrigerate for at least 4 hours or until ready to serve. Serve chilled, with sour cream on the side.

Chilled Cherry Soup

This is another soup that is quick, elegant, and most unusual. It is ideal for a Passover dessert, since it helps use up any leftover wine. At other times of the year, substitute cornstarch for the potato starch.

If this soup is served at a dairy meal, add a dollop of sour cream to each serving; if it is a dessert, substitute whipped cream or vanilla ice cream.

pareve; with sour cream: dairy
kosher for Passover

SERVES 8

2 pounds fresh black cherries, or 2 cans (14-ounce each) pitted sweet cherries	1/4 cup sugar
	2 tablespoons potato starch
3 to 4 cups water	1 cup sweet red wine
3 whole cloves	juice and grated rind of 1 lemon
1 stick cinnamon	

If you are using fresh cherries, trim and wash, then pit them. Put pitted cherries in a large pot with 4 cups water, and add the spices and sugar. Bring to a boil over high heat, then reduce heat and simmer until the cherries are tender, about 10 minutes.

If you are using canned cherries, drain and put them in a large pot, add 3 cups water, the spices, and sugar, and set over medium heat. Heat to just below boiling point.

Put the potato starch into a small bowl, add the wine, and stir to dissolve. Add the lemon juice and rind. Remove the pot from the heat and stir in the potato-starch mixture. Return the pot to the heat and cook, stirring constantly, until the liquid thickens.

Let the soup cool, then transfer it to a nonmetal container. Cover with plastic wrap and chill until ready to serve.

Israeli Fruit Soup

This soup originates from the Baltic States and Scandinavia, but it has become a staple of the Israeli diet. It is more often eaten as a dessert than as a first course, but it is still a soup. Other fruit, such as blueberries or boysenberries, which are not available in Israel, can greatly enhance the flavor of a fruit soup, so don't be afraid to change the fruit combination to suit your tastes. Remember that fresh fruits absorb less water than dried. It is not necessary to peel the apples.

pareve, kosher for Passover

SERVES 8

1 cup pitted prunes, or 2 cups pitted and diced fresh plums
½ cup chopped dried apricots, or ½ cup pitted and chopped fresh apricots
1 cup cored and chopped apples
½ cup chopped dried peaches, or 1 cup pitted and chopped fresh peaches

½ cup golden raisins
juice and grated rind of 1 lemon
2 quarts + 1 cup water
1 tablespoon potato starch or cornstarch

If you are using fresh fruits, sprinkle them with the lemon juice immediately upon cutting to prevent discoloring.

Place the fruits, lemon juice, and grated rind in a large pot and add 2 quarts water. Bring to a boil over high heat, then reduce the heat, cover, and simmer at a gentle bubble for 1 hour.

Remove the pot from the heat. Combine the potato or cornstarch with remaining 1 cup water and stir to dissolve. Add starch mixture to the soup, stirring well. Place the pot over medium heat and cook, stirring constantly, until soup thickens slightly. Transfer soup to a nonmetal container and let cool. Cover with plastic wrap, then refrigerate until ready to serve.

4

EGG DISHES

Eggs, like fish, are animal products that are neither milk nor meat, so they are useful additions to many dishes. Scrambled eggs, omelets, and pancakes are very popular throughout the Jewish world.

The egg also has a certain symbolism, which is why it is eaten at Passover. It signifies the life cycle, so it is a symbol of both rebirth and mourning, thus eggs are traditional at either birth celebrations or funerals. They are eaten in vast quantities on the 8 days of Passover, during which they also symbolize Spring.

Sweet-and-Sour Eggs

This Polish recipe makes a good appetizer as well as a snack. I first had these eggs while visiting a Polish family in Tel-Aviv. The head of the household, who was in his eighties, kept washing them down with tiny glasses of various flavored vodkas which he had made himself!

pareve

SERVES 4

4 hard-cooked eggs
1 cup olive oil
1 cup cider vinegar
1 onion, finely chopped

1 teaspoon salt
½ teaspoon black pepper
1 teaspoon sugar

Slice the eggs lengthwise into quarters. Place egg quarters in a shallow dish. Combine remaining ingredients in a bowl. Pour the liquid over the eggs and refrigerate, lightly covered with plastic, for 24 hours.

To serve, arrange the eggs on a serving dish and sprinkle them with a little of the marinade. Serve with Chrein (page 184).

Hamindas

These slow-cooked eggs are typical of Sephardic cooking. They are often simmered in a stew (see Dfina, page 85), but they can also be cooked separately. The slow cooking makes them especially delicious, and they are an excellent picnic food.

The onion skins are the papery brown coverings of yellow onions, not the white inner layers. Eggs can also be cooked in oil and Turkish coffee grounds, which will give them a similar delicious flavor and attractive color.

pareve, kosher for Passover

SERVES 8

8 eggs in their shells
skins of 8 yellow onions

4 tablespoons oil
¼ teaspoon black pepper

Preheat oven to 350°F. Wrap the eggs loosely in the onion skins. Place them in a small ovenproof casserole with a lid. Add water to cover by about ½ inch, then add the oil and pepper. Cover casserole tightly and place in oven. Reduce the heat to minimum (about 250°F) and bake for 8 hours or overnight. Serve next day for lunch with salad or as an appetizer.

Egg and Onion

You'd better like onions! This dish really should be called "Onion and Egg." Eat it with pumpernickel or sour rye bread. It is an appetizer popular in eastern Poland and Russia, where even the most strongly flavored onions are eaten raw as if they were apples.

pareve, kosher for Passover

SERVES 4 TO 6

6 tablespoons shortening
2 pounds white onions, chopped

6 hard-cooked eggs
salt and black pepper

Melt the shortening and sauté the onions until browned. Chop the hard-cooked eggs and mix well with the onions. Sprinkle mixture with any shortening remaining in the pan and season to taste. Serve warm.

Egg and Tomato Scramble

This breakfast dish, called *shakshooka*, was brought to Israel by Tunisian Jews. They like it very hot, but you can adjust the amount of chili pepper to suit your palate. The tomato mixture can be made in advance and reheated before adding the eggs.

pareve

SERVES 4 TO 6

¼ cup margarine
3 pounds tomatoes, peeled and chopped
1 teaspoon chili powder, or to taste
1 tablespoon all-purpose flour

3 eggs
½ teaspoon salt
4 to 6 pita breads

Melt the margarine in a deep skillet or saucepan over medium heat. Add the tomatoes and their juice, then add the chili powder and flour and stir until smooth. Reduce heat and simmer, uncovered, very gently for 1 hour. Beat eggs with salt in a small bowl. Just before serving, add the egg mixture to the tomatoes and stir lightly. Serve hot, with pita bread.

Matzo Brei

Although Matzo Brei can also be served sweet with sugar and cinnamon, I prefer it as a savory luncheon dish, with plain boiled potatoes.

dairy, kosher for Passover

SERVES 2

2 whole matzos
½ cup milk
2 eggs, well beaten

salt and black pepper
2 tablespoons butter

Place the matzos in a large, shallow dish and cover with the milk. Drain well and transfer to a bowl. Stir in the eggs, salt, and pepper.

Heat the butter in a skillet over moderate heat. Add the egg mixture and cover the pan. Cook for about 10 minutes, or until the underside is well browned. Turn carefully and brown the other side. Serve at once.

Potato-Mushroom Pancakes

Pancakes are very popular in Central and Eastern Europe, packed with sweet or savory fillings. (Sweet pancakes are included in the desserts chapter.) The pancake batter is made without milk so that the filling can contain meat, if desired. The potato and mushroom filling here is typical, but is only an example. Leftovers of almost any kind can be chopped and used to fill the pancakes; for instance, use chopped spinach, cooked potato moistened with a little gravy or white sauce, and so on. If the filling is meat, or if the pancakes are to be eaten at a meat meal, substitute margarine or shortening for the butter in the batter.

batter: pareve; filling: dairy

SERVES 6 TO 8

BATTER
4 eggs
2 cups all-purpose flour
1 cup + 2 tablespoons water
½ teaspoon salt
1 teaspoon oil
1 teaspoon butter

FILLING
1 tablespoon butter
1 large onion, finely chopped

8 ounces fresh mushrooms, chopped
5 large potatoes, peeled, boiled, and
    mashed
salt and black pepper
1 egg, lightly beaten

TOPPING
4 tablespoons grated cheese, or 4 table-
    spoons breadcrumbs combined with 4
    tablespoons melted butter

For the batter, break the eggs into a mixing bowl. Add the flour, oil, and 2 tablespoons water. Beat well until mixture is smooth, gradually adding remaining cup of water. Batter should be the consistency of single cream. Stir in the salt. Cover the bowl with a cloth and let batter rest at room temperature for at least 30 minutes.

To make the pancakes, rub the butter lightly over the surface of a nonstick crêpe pan or heavy skillet. Heat the pan over high heat, and when it is hot, add about 2 tablespoons of the batter, tilting the pan to spread it evenly over the surface. Cook, shaking the pan, until the pancake no longer sticks to it, about 3 minutes. Wait a couple of seconds, then turn the pancake over. Cook about 1 minute on the other side, then lay pancake on absorbent paper, and repeat with the rest of the mixture.

To make the filling, melt the butter in a saucepan over high heat and cook the onion until it is transparent. Add the mushrooms, cover, and cook on low heat until mushrooms give up their juices, about 10 minutes.

Place the mashed potatoes in a large bowl. Pour the contents of the saucepan over the potatoes. Add the egg and stir well. Season and use the mixture to stuff the pancakes.

To fill the pancakes, lay a tablespoon of filling down the center of a pancake. Fold the short sides toward the filling and then fold over the longer sides to encase the filling. Continue with rest of pancakes.

Preheat broiler. Arrange the pancakes in a greased ovenproof dish. Sprinkle the pancakes with either the cheese or the breadcrumb mixture and place in broiler to brown, about 3 minutes. Serve at once.

PASSOVER VARIATION

Substitute 2 cups fine matzo meal for the flour in the batter. Sprinkle filled pancakes with a mixture of Matzo Farfel (page 53) and melted butter instead of the breadcrumbs.

Sabzi Kuku

This is a delicious Persian dish, an herb pancake traditional at Shavuot, but just as popular any other time of year. It is from Hannah Levy, who brought it with her from Meshhed, Iran. She points out that any herbs and suitable greens can be used, and the combination varies depending on the season. In Iran, the greens are ground in a mortar with a pestle, but a food processor also does a fine job.

pareve, kosher for Passover

SERVES 4

4 cups chopped spinach or Swiss chard	6 eggs
2 sprigs each fresh parsley, coriander, and dill	salt and black pepper
	1 cup matzo meal
2 leeks, thinly sliced	4 tablespoons oil

Grind the greens and herbs in a food processor until smooth; you may have to do it in a couple of batches. Combine in a large bowl with the eggs, then season to taste. Stir in the matzo meal. If the mixture is too stiff to drop easily from a spoon, add a little water. It should have the consistency of thick cream.

Heat the oil in a skillet over high heat. When oil is very hot, drop 1 or 2 tablespoons of the mixture into the pan to make pancakes about 3 inches in diameter. Cook 2 minutes, then turn them and cook another 2 minutes. Drain the pancakes on absorbent paper, and continue to make more until batter is used up. Serve warm or cold with cream or cottage cheese.

5

DUMPLINGS, PASTA, GRAINS, AND RICE

Pasta and dumplings are used in 2 ways in Jewish cookery: They are added to soups or they are fried and served as substitutes for potatoes as an accompaniment to the entree. Like appetizers, these flour-based foods are served as fillers to make up for a smaller meat course, but this does not mean they are not delicious in their own right. You will notice that most of these recipes are Ashkenazic. That is because most of the Sephardic Jews have been lucky enough to live in countries where the winters are so mild they do not need heavy, filling foods to keep them warm.

Pasta is popular throughout the Jewish world. The Sephardic communities tend to eat pasta as a rice substitute and, of course, it is popular among Italian Jews. Pasta has a very ancient Mediterranean origin. It is mentioned in the Jerusalem Talmud (Tractate Betza 9), and the eminent food historian Charles Perry believes it actually originated in the eastern Mediterranean, in Roman provinces such as Judaea. Dare one suggest that the Romans brought it thence to Italy?

Lokshen, Itriot, Rishta, and *Fideos* are the names—in Yiddish, Hebrew, Arabic, and Judezmo respectively—for the noodle. Basically, 2 widths of noodle are used: medium-wide, known as *tagliatelle* or *fettuccine* in Italian; and thin, stringlike, known as *vermicelli*. Vermicelli (called *fideos* in Judezmo) are the commonest type of noodle in Sephardic and Middle Eastern Jewish dishes. Macaroni is also a popular dish on Jewish tables in Greece and Turkey. I've included recipes for making your own pasta, but you can substitute commercial in some instances. Remember that fresh noodles need only one-fourth the cooking time of package noodles.

Rice occupies the same important place in Sephardic and Middle Eastern food as it does in China and other parts of the Far East. For this reason, rice is permitted on Passover among Sephardic and Middle Eastern communities, though pasta (unless made with matzo flour) is not kosher for Passover in any community.

Fresh Noodle Dough

pareve

SERVES 4 TO 6

2 cups all-purpose flour

1 egg

2 tablespoons water

½ teaspoon salt

Sift the flour onto a board and make a well in the center. Add the egg, water, and salt. Mix until the dough forms a ball. It should be very stiff, but if it will not stick together, you may have to add an extra teaspoon of water. Knead well until the dough is smooth and elastic, about 10 minutes. Shape into a ball, cover with plastic wrap, and refrigerate for 1 hour.

Roll out the dough on a floured board until paper thin, and leave it to dry for about 30 minutes. To slice the dough, either use a pasta machine, or roll it up like a jelly roll, and slice it crosswise at ¼-inch or ¹⁄₁₆-inch intervals, depending on whether you want wide or thin noodles. Shake the noodles to separate them, and hang them over a rack (or horizontal broom handle supported by 2 chairs) to dry in a warm, dry place, up to 3 to 4 hours.

When noodles are completely dry, store in a jar with a tight-fitting lid; they will keep as long as packaged noodles. To cook, place noodles in rapidly boiling salted water: 5 minutes for thick, 2 minutes for thin. Add noodles to boiling soup or use in noodle dishes.

Fresh Orzo

This is the Greek name for a type of pasta which resembles grains of rice. It is very popular in Egypt, where it is known as *lissan al-asfoor* (birds' tongues).

pareve

SERVES 4 TO 6

2 cups fine semolina (farina)
½ teaspoon salt

2 tablespoons vegetable oil
all-purpose flour for dusting

Put the semolina in a large bowl. Add the salt, oil, and enough warm water to make a stiff dough. Cover with a cloth and let rest at room temperature for at least 15 minutes.

Knead the dough thoroughly on a floured board for 15 minutes or until it is smooth and elastic. (This can also be done in a food processor or mixer, using bread-kneading attachments.) Shape dough into a long, thin rope about ½ inch in diameter. Use a small, sharp knife to cut it into small pieces, each about half the size of a coffee bean. Spread these little pieces of dough on a clean cloth and let dry in a warm, well-aired place for at least 2 hours. Once dry, store in an airtight container until ready to use. Add to soups as desired. Orzo needs only 5 minutes cooking time in boiling water or broth.

Farfel

Farfel derives from the Italian word *farfalla*, meaning butterfly, because of the butterfly shape of these tiny pieces of pasta. It can be bought ready for cooking or you can make it from scratch.

Farfel is very versatile. It can be used as an addition to soup, as a side dish to accompany the main course, or to make a Schaleth (see page 128).

pareve

SERVES 4 TO 6

1 recipe Fresh Noodle Dough (page 51)
all-purpose flour for dusting
2 tablespoons shortening

½ teaspoon salt
½ teaspoon paprika

Prepare the noodle dough and roll it out until it is ⅛ inch thick. Cut dough into ¼-inch strips, then sprinkle strips with more flour. Using a large, sharp knife, chop strips into little pieces the size of grains of rice. (This can also be done in a food processor.) Spread pieces to dry on paper towels, either in a warm place or in an oven with a pilot light or on its lowest setting, about 2 hours. When dry, store farfel in an airtight container until you are ready to use it.

To cook farfel as a side dish, melt the shortening in a skillet. Add the farfel, in batches if necessary, to ensure that it can be turned easily to coat with shortening. Stir constantly, taking care to not crush the pieces. When the farfel is an even, golden color, sprinkle with salt and paprika. The farfel will swell while cooking. Serve hot.

Matzo Farfel

During Passover, farfel can be made with matzo meal. Choose fine meal, also known as cake meal.

pareve, kosher for Passover

SERVES 4 TO 6

2 cups matzo meal
½ teaspoon salt

2 eggs, lightly beaten
matzo meal for dusting

Sift the matzo meal and salt into a large bowl. Add the eggs and work mixture into a stiff dough. Roll out dough until ⅛ inch thick and cut into ¼-inch strips. Sprinkle the strips with more matzo meal. Using a large, sharp knife, chop strips into little pieces the size of grains of rice. (This can also be done in a food processor.) Spread the grains to dry on paper towels for 2 hours, either in a warm place or in an oven with a pilot light.

When dry, store the grains in an airtight jar or tin. Use them like plain Farfel (see page 52).

Noodle Kugel

This is the traditional accompaniment to the Sabbath stew, cooked overnight in a very slow oven and served at lunch on Saturday.

meat, can be slow-cooked for Sabbath

SERVES 8

½ cup dry breadcrumbs
8 ounces noodles, cooked and drained
¾ cup chicken fat or shortening

½ teaspoon salt
½ teaspoon black pepper
2 eggs, lightly beaten

Preheat oven to 450°F. Grease a 2-quart casserole or baking dish and sprinkle with the breadcrumbs. Combine remaining ingredients in a large bowl, then pour into prepared dish and cover tightly with foil.

Bake for 30 minutes, then reduce the heat to 375°F, and bake another 30 minutes. Reduce heat further to about 200°F and cook for at least 4 more hours. Serve with stew or other meats.

Pharaoh's Wheel Noodles

This Italian dish symbolizes the passage of the Jews across the Red Sea. The name recalls how the Pharaoh was crushed beneath his chariot wheel. There are several versions of this, but all include pasta, sauce, salami, and raisins. (Italian Jews make a wonderful goose salami.)

Make your own meat or tomato sauce, or follow the stuffing mixture in Georgian Chicken (page 98) but omit the sweet spices and almonds, and instead add 4 peeled tomatoes or enough tomato sauce to make more liquid.

This dish tastes very special, thanks to the raisins and pine nuts, yet all the ingredients are precooked or need no additional cooking, so it is also simple and quick to prepare.

meat

SERVES 6

1 package (8 ounces) egg noodles,
  cooked until al dente
2 cups Italian meat sauce

8 ounces kosher salami, thinly sliced
½ cup raisins
½ cup pine nuts (pignolis)

Preheat the oven to 400°F. Grease a 2-quart round, glass baking dish. Arrange a layer of cooked noodles in the dish, then pour some of the sauce over them. Arrange a ring of salami round the edge of the dish, and sprinkle some raisins and pine nuts in the center. Add another layer of pasta and repeat the sauce, salami, raisins, and pine nuts. Continue layering until all the ingredients are used up, finishing with a layer of salami. Bake for 20 minutes, or until heated through. Serve immediately.

Kreplach

These are Jewish ravioli, very similar to the *man-tou* or *manty* stuffed dumplings eaten from Eastern Europe to China. The name *kreplach* is a Yiddish diminutive of the French word *crêpe*—i.e., "little crêpe." Yiddish words of French origin date back to the early Middle Ages when there were large Jewish communities in the Rhineland (then part of France).

pareve

MAKES 50

KREPLACH DOUGH
2 cups all-purpose flour
½ teaspoon salt

2 eggs, lightly beaten
2 tablespoons cold water
additional flour for dusting

To make the dough, sift the flour and salt into a bowl. Make a well in the center and put in the eggs and water. Gradually incorporate the flour into the eggs until you have a stiff dough. Cover bowl and let dough rest while you prepare desired filling.

When ready to fill, roll out the dough until ¹⁄₁₆ inch thick on a lightly floured work surface. Use a ravioli cutter or sharp knife to cut the dough into 2-inch squares. Place a heaping teaspoon of filling in the center of each square. Fold the dough over the filling to form a triangle. Wet your fingers and pinch the edges of the dough firmly together to prevent filling from escaping.

To cook filled kreplach, drop them into boiling salted water or soup and cook for 15 minutes. Drain well if they are to be served separately.

Potato and Mushroom Filling

If you cannot find imported dried mushrooms, substitute fresh button mushrooms but do not soak them.

pareve

10 potatoes, boiled in their skins
2 tablespoons shortening
2 onions, finely chopped
2 ounces dried mushrooms, soaked in
   warm water for 10 minutes

½ teaspoon salt
½ teaspoon black pepper

Peel and mash the potatoes. Melt the shortening in a skillet over high heat and sauté the onions until lightly browned. Set aside. Drain the mushrooms and briefly sauté them in the remaining shortening. Mix the mashed potatoes, sautéed onions, and sautéed mushrooms, then season mixture with salt and pepper. These kreplach are equally good in meatless soups or sautéed and served at a nonmeat meal.

Meat Filling

Meat-filled kreplach are traditionally eaten in soups on Purim, at the last meal before the Yom Kippur fast, and on Hoshanah Rabbah. An Ashkenazic tradition is that kreplach have hidden ingredients (the filling), and that the 3 occasions in question have mysterious characteristics whose meaning is hidden from us.

meat

1 onion, finely chopped	2 cups ground or chopped boiled beef
2 tablespoons water	½ teaspoon salt
2 tablespoons chicken fat	½ teaspoon black pepper

Put the onion and water into a small saucepan over medium heat. Cover the pan and cook the onion until it is soft, about 5 minutes. Melt the chicken fat in a skillet over high heat. Mix the remaining ingredients in a bowl, then add to skillet and sauté the mixture until the meat loses its redness, stirring constantly to break up any lumps, about 7 minutes. Let cool before using to fill the kreplach.

Sautéed Cheese Kreplach

Kreplach are eaten on Shavuot, the Feast of Weeks, so-called because it falls 7 weeks after Passover. Since it is the time of year when cows' and ewes' milk is most abundant, it is a farming tradition in many countries to eat milk dishes and those made from uncured cheeses. The eating of dairy foods on Shavuot is another reminder that the Jews were originally a nation of farmers and shepherds. The festival is also called *Hag Habikurim*—the Festival of First Fruits. It was the time when the barley harvest and the first summer fruits were brought to the Temple in Jerusalem.

The grated cheddar cheese in this recipe gives the Cheese Kreplach a little extra "bite."

dairy

SERVES 6 TO 8

1 batch Kreplach Dough (recipe page 55)	½ teaspoon salt
	½ cup butter, melted
1 pound cottage cheese	1 cup sour cream or thick plain yogurt
½ cup grated cheddar cheese	½ teaspoon paprika
2 eggs, lightly beaten	

Make the kreplach dough. Combine the cottage cheese, cheddar cheese, eggs, and salt in a bowl. Use the mixture to fill the kreplach, then cook kreplach in boiling, salted water for 15 minutes.

Drain the kreplach on absorbent paper. Melt 2 tablespoons of the butter in a skillet and sauté a few kreplach until lightly browned, about 3 minutes on each side. As they are cooked, pile them onto a plate and keep warm. Use remaining butter to sauté rest of kreplach in small batches. Pour some of the sour cream or yogurt over the kreplach, and serve the remainder separately. Sprinkle the kreplach with the paprika, then serve as a main course for a dairy meal.

Potato Dumplings

Dumplings are popular throughout Central and Eastern Europe. Although they can still be eaten in the homes of German Jewish immigrants, their popularity is waning in America. This is a pity, because they are delicious and original. To vary the flavor, add a tablespoon of caraway seeds to the dumpling mixture.

pareve

SERVES 8

4 large potatoes, boiled in their skins
4 egg yolks
½ cup cold water
½ teaspoon salt

¼ teaspoon black pepper
¼ teaspoon grated nutmeg
4 tablespoons all-purpose flour

Peel and mash the potatoes. Beat the egg yolks with cold water and combine with the potatoes. Add the salt, pepper, and nutmeg. Stir in enough of the flour to make a firm dough.

Bring a large pot of salted water to a boil over high heat. With floured hands, shape the dough into small balls. Drop a few balls at a time into water and poach for 10 minutes. Drain. Continue cooking remaining dumplings. Serve with stew.

Mrs. Levy's Matzo Cleis

Matzo balls are perhaps the quintessential example of Jewish food in this book. There are almost as many recipes for matzo balls as there are Jewish cooks. I include but a sampling here. Matzo balls are always served in soup, usually chicken soup. They are traditional at Passover, though equally popular at other times of the year.

This first recipe (using the original spelling) is adapted from the oldest American Jewish cookbook, published in Philadelphia in 1871 and written by Mrs. Esther Levy née Jacobs. It bears a strong resemblance to the matzo balls made by my great-grandmother, Amelia Shmith.

pareve, kosher for Passover

MAKES 30

2 matzos	2 tablespoons chopped fresh parsley
2 tablespoons oil	½ teaspoon salt
2 onions, chopped	½ teaspoon black pepper
3 eggs, lightly beaten	⅛ teaspoon ground ginger
½ cup matzo meal	⅛ teaspoon ground nutmeg

Soak the matzos in water to cover. While they are soaking, heat the oil in a skillet over high heat and sauté the onions until they are transparent but do not let them brown.

Squeeze the excess moisture from the matzos, and put them into a large bowl. Add the eggs, matzo meal, parsley, salt, pepper, ginger, and nutmeg. Stir, then add the onion and mix well.

Wet your hands and form the mixture into balls the size of a walnut (some people prefer a larger size). Drop the balls into soup that is just below boiling point and cook on very low heat for 10 minutes.

Kneidlach

This is the matzo ball recipe I usually use myself. It is based on my mother's and grandmother's recipes, and is very light and fluffy. The secret is to keep the soup just below boiling point.

meat, kosher for Passover

MAKES 25

1 cup medium matzo meal	2 tablespoons chicken fat
1 cup boiling water	½ teaspoon salt
2 tablespoons ground almonds	½ teaspoon black pepper
1 egg, lightly beaten	¼ teaspoon ground ginger

Pour boiling water over the matzo meal in a bowl and stir until well blended. Add the rest of the ingredients, mix well, and chill for at least 1 hour.

Wet your hands and make 1-inch balls with the mixture. Drop balls into boiling soup and simmer on very gentle heat, uncovered, for 15 minutes.

Nockerl

These egg dumplings were a favorite among Jews in Austria and Hungary, and are eaten wherever Jews from these countries are living.

pareve

MAKES 30

2 eggs	½ cup all-purpose flour
½ cup water	½ teaspoon baking powder
1 teaspoon salt	

Stuffed Cabbage Rolls; recipe on page 88

Place the eggs and the water in a bowl. Add the salt and beat well. Stir in the flour and baking powder, and beat until smooth.

Drop teaspoons of the mixture into boiling, salted water or soup. Cook until the nockerl rise to the surface, then remove them immediately with a slotted spoon. Serve with a hearty stew, such as a goulash.

Sabbath Kugel

No Sabbath midday meal in Poland or Russia was complete without a kugel. The very slow cooking of this type of pudding turns the starch into dextrin, giving it a unique flavor. It is not possible to hurry a kugel—however minimum cooking times are possible. The kugel is traditionally baked with the cholent (see page 84), often in a special compartment of the same pot.

meat, can be slow-cooked for Sabbath

SERVES 6

½ cup fine dry breadcrumbs	2 eggs, lightly beaten
2 cups all-purpose flour	½ teaspoon salt
8 ounces chicken fat or shortening	½ teaspoon black pepper

Preheat the oven to 450°F. Grease a 2-quart mold or baking dish and sprinkle it evenly with the dry breadcrumbs. Combine the flour, fat, and eggs in a bowl, then season with salt and pepper. Add the mixture to prepared dish and cover with a double thickness of foil. Secure the foil tightly. Bake the pudding for 30 minutes, then reduce the heat to 375°F and let it bake for an additional 2 hours.

Remove the kugel from the oven, remove the foil, and unmold onto a plate. Slide kugel from the plate back into the dish so that the side that was on top is now underneath. Cover again with foil and return dish to oven. Reduce the heat to 250°F and bake for at least 4 more hours, or overnight. Serve with cholent.

Passover Kugel

meat, kosher for Passover
can be slow-cooked for Sabbath

SERVES 8

10 matzos
¾ cup chicken fat or shortening
2 eggs, lightly beaten

½ teaspoon salt
pinch of sugar
½ cup fine matzo meal

Preheat oven to 450°F. Grease a 2-quart baking dish.

Soak the matzos in water until soft, then squeeze them dry; place in bowl. Chop the chicken fat into the matzos much as you would cut fat into flour for a pie crust. Add the beaten eggs, salt, and sugar. Mix well, then pour into prepared dish. Cover tightly with foil. Bake for 30 minutes, then reduce the heat to 375°F and bake for an additional hour.

Unmold the kugel and turn it upside down, as described in the previous recipe. Return kugel to oven. Reduce heat to 250°F and bake for at least 4 hours or overnight. Serve with cholent.

Malai

This savory cheese pudding from Romania is served as an accompaniment to fish or pareve dishes, or as a dairy entree. This is a very good dish to bake in a microwave, in which case there is no need to butter the baking dish.

dairy

SERVES 8

½ cake compressed yeast, or 1 package
    active dry yeast
3½ cups lukewarm water
2 teaspoons sugar
½ cup all-purpose flour
2 cups yellow cornmeal

1 teaspoon salt
1 cup pot or farmer cheese, drained
6 green onions, sliced
½ teaspoon black pepper
3 tablespoons butter, melted

In a large bowl, dissolve the yeast in ½ cup lukewarm water, add half the sugar, and leave in a warm place for 20 minutes, or until foaming.

Add the flour to the yeast mixture and mix well. Cover with plastic wrap and let rise in a warm place for about 1 hour.

Preheat oven to 350°F. Generously butter a 2-quart baking dish.

Add the cornmeal, salt, remaining sugar, and remaining 3 cups lukewarm water to the batter. Mix well; batter should be as thick as mayonnaise.

Mash the cheese with a fork until smooth, then stir in onions. Pour half the batter into a prepared baking dish. Cover with the cheese mixture, then add rest of batter. Drizzle on melted butter. Bake for 45 minutes or until firm and browned on top.

Mamaliga

Here is another famous Romanian cornmeal dish. Mamaliga is similar to the polenta of northern Italy, and it is typical of the Romanian Jewish diet. It is combined here with cottage cheese to make a pudding.

It is most important that you stir the cornmeal as it cooks. In northern Italy and Romania, cooks use a long wooden pole to stir, but a wooden spoon works well, too. When served cold, the mamaliga is sliced with a cotton thread.

dairy

SERVES 8

2 cups yellow cornmeal
1 cup cold water
1 teaspoon salt

½ cup butter
2 cups cottage cheese, drained and sieved

Mix the cornmeal is a bowl with cold water until you have a smooth paste. Bring 1 quart of water to a boil in a large pan. Add salt, then gradually sprinkle in the cornmeal, stirring constantly to prevent lumps. Cook over low heat, stirring steadily for 30 minutes. When the water has been absorbed and the cornmeal is soft, it is ready. Lightly stir in the butter and cottage cheese. Serve hot or cold.

Kasha with Mushrooms

Kasha is to the Russians and Poles what cornmeal is to the Romanians. Properly cooked kasha grains should be fluffy yet separate; when the cooking is finished, no liquid should be visible in the pan.

pareve

SERVES 4 TO 6

1 cup sliced fresh mushrooms	1 egg, lightly beaten
1 teaspoon lemon juice	½ teaspoon salt
1 tablespoon margarine	¼ teaspoon black pepper
1 cup kasha	2 cups vegetable broth or hot water

Sprinkle the cut mushrooms with the lemon juice. Melt the margarine in a saucepan over low heat, add the mushrooms, and cover. Simmer gently, until the mushrooms give up their liquid. Set aside.

Place kasha in a bowl and stir in the egg. When the grains are thoroughly coated with egg, transfer kasha to a heavy skillet with a lid. Sprinkle with salt and pepper. Place the skillet over high heat and cook kasha, stirring constantly with a spatula, until the grains separate—about 2 to 4 minutes.

Remove the pan from the heat and add the vegetable broth and mushrooms. Stir well, then reduce the heat, return the pan to stove, and cover. Simmer 10 minutes, then remove the lid, stir kasha, and leave on low heat for 3 to 5 minutes or until all the liquid has been absorbed. Serve as an accompaniment to the entree.

Kasha Varnishkes

There are 2 approaches to this Ukrainian dish. In the simplest, the kasha is cooked with an equal quantity of bowtie or shell pastas, which are parboiled and added 5 minutes before the kasha finishes cooking. In the more authentic version, the kasha is used as a filling inside little turnovers called *varnishkes*, the Yiddish version of the Russian *vareniki*.

pareve

SERVES 6 TO 8

1 batch Fresh Noodle Dough (page 51)   *Kasha with Mushrooms (page 64)*

Roll out noodle dough ⅛ inch thick to form a rectangle. Use a cookie cutter or glass to cut the dough into 3-inch circles. Place a teaspoonful of kasha filling in the center of each circle, and fold the circles in half. Press the edges together with the tines of a fork to seal them shut.

Bring a large quantity of salted water to a boil over high heat, then add turnovers. Cook for 15 minutes, then drain. Serve hot with meat or mushrooms. If desired, briefly fry the varnishkes in margarine and serve with vegetables and sour cream as a main dish.

Kishka

This Polish dish is a kind of sausage, but it is included with grains because the only meat in it is the skin. Few people bother to make sausages at home nowadays, but if you have a sausage-making attachment on your mixer and have never used it, here is your chance. Beef sausage casings are available on request from your kosher butcher, or he can tell you where to get them. Casings are always sold prekoshered.

meat

SERVES 4

12 inches of koshered beef sausage casing
2 cups all-purpose flour
8 ounces beef kidney fat or shortening,
  chopped

½ teaspoon salt
½ teaspoon black pepper
½ teaspoon paprika

Turn the sausage casing inside out, so the shiny side faces outward, and kosher it in the usual way (unless it has already been koshered). Cut the fat into the flour as you would to make a pie crust. Season mixture with salt, pepper, and paprika.

Tie a knot in one end of the casing. Fill it loosely with the mixture, taking care not to stuff the sausage too tight or it will burst. Leave about ¼ inch unfilled at the top and make a second knot at the other end.

Bring a large pot of salted water to a boil over high heat. When it boils, add the kishka. Reduce the heat so that the water barely moves, and poach the sausage at just below boiling point for 1½ hours.

When the kishka is ready, serve at once or refrigerate for a day or two. When ready to serve, fry or cook it with cholent and serve with Farfel (page 52).

Stuffed Neck (Derma)

The neck used in this preparation was once a goose neck, during a time when geese were plentiful. Nowadays, chicken neck skins are used. This is the stuffed neck my Polish Grandma Bessie used to make for me when as a little girl I came to Sunday lunch. Of course, the amount of ingredients can be a problem, since necks tend to vary in length. I've provided enough stuffing for the longest of chicken necks.

meat, kosher for Passover

SERVES 4

1 neck skin of chicken
½ cup ground almonds
1 tablespoon matzo meal
2 tablespoons chopped fresh parsley
1 egg, lightly beaten
½ teaspoon salt
½ teaspoon black pepper
½ teaspoon ground allspice

Stuffed neck is usually an accompaniment to a roast chicken, so plan on baking it as you also cook your roast. You should have oven set on medium heat (350°F). Check that there are no holes in the neck skin, other than at either end. Sew up one end of the neck.

In a bowl, mix the stuffing ingredients well. Fill the neck skin with mixture, packing fairly tightly (any extra stuffing can be used to stuff the bird). Sew up the other end of the neck, then place it in the oven alongside your roast. Roast it with the bird. Turn it once or twice during cooking to brown it evenly. When ready, slice neck crosswise into ½-inch pieces and serve as an accompaniment to the roast.

Riso Giallo

Saffron rice is a traditional Friday evening dish among the Jews of Ferrara in Italy. Italian Jews can claim to be the oldest permanently settled community in the Diaspora. There have been Jews in Rome since Roman times; consequently, they have their own special traditions and customs, and are neither Sephardic nor Ashkenazic, though both Ashkenazic and Sephardic Jews have established communities in Italy.

meat

SERVES 8

6 tablespoons olive oil
2 cups long-grain rice
3 cups hot chicken or veal broth

1 teaspoon saffron strands
½ teaspoon salt
½ teaspoon black pepper

Heat the oil in a large saucepan over high heat. Add the rice and cook, stirring constantly with a wooden spoon to coat each grain, until the rice starts to pop and leap in the pan. Add 2 cups of the broth. Cover the pan and cook for 7 minutes or until the broth has been absorbed.

Dissolve the saffron strands in the remaining broth. When the broth has been absorbed, add the saffron-colored broth. Reduce heat and cook, covered, until liquid has been absorbed. Stir well and season to taste. Remove rice from the heat and spread on a serving platter, around a roast or on its own. The rice is normally served warm, but not hot.

Turkish Pilaf

Like saffron rice, this dish can also be served lukewarm, or even cold. It is a rice dish served on special occasions, such as Friday nights and festivals. Turkey is famous for its apricots, golden raisins, and pistachio nuts—all of which are exported to the United States. Rinse the rice ahead of time to remove excess starch. Photo opposite page 76.

pareve

SERVES 8

2½ tablespoons oil
2 cups long-grain rice
1 quart water
½ teaspoon salt

¼ cup split blanched almonds
¼ cup shelled pistachio nuts
¼ cup golden raisins
¼ cup chopped dried apricots

Heat 2 tablespoons of the oil in a large saucepan over high heat. Add the rice and cook, stirring constantly with a wooden spoon, until all the grains are coated. Add water and salt and cover the pan with a cloth, then with the lid. Reduce the heat to a simmer and cook for 15 minutes.

Meanwhile, toast the almonds in a dry, nonstick skillet. When they start to give off their characteristic aroma—in about 5 minutes—they are ready. Remove the rice from the heat; it should have absorbed all the liquid. If not, return rice to the heat uncovered for a few minutes to finish evaporation. Transfer rice to a large bowl and stir in the almonds, pistachios, raisins, and apricots.

Serve the rice heaped in a mound on a serving platter; or press it into a ring mold brushed with oil, then unmold to give rice an attractive shape on a platter. Decorate with sprigs of fresh greens, such as coriander leaves (cilantro), watercress, or mâche.

Sephardic Sabbath Rice

This savory baked rice pudding would be cooked like a *kugel* along with the Sabbath stew. It is kosher for Passover for Sephardic Jews only.

4 tablespoons chicken fat or shortening
2 onions, chopped
3 cups cooked long-grain rice

½ teaspoon salt
½ teaspoon black pepper
2 eggs, lightly beaten

meat, can be slow-cooked for Sabbath

SERVES 6 TO 8

Melt the fat in a large skillet set over high heat and sauté the onions until they are golden. Set aside.

Preheat oven to 250°F. Lightly grease a 1-quart baking dish. Place rice in a large bowl. Stir in the onions and cooking fat. Add the salt, pepper, and beaten eggs and mix well. Transfer mixture to the baking dish, and cover tightly with foil. Bake overnight, then serve for Sabbath lunch.

Persian Rice

The latest Jewish community to suffer from persecution is the one in Iran. Almost the entire Jewish community there has disappeared. Fortunately, most have survived, resettling all over the world. Many Iranian Jews have come to live in Los Angeles, and this recipe belongs to Hannah Fereydoun of Beverly Hills. Also called *chello*, it is unique.

pareve

SERVES 6 TO 8

2 cups long-grain rice
6½ cups water

1 teaspoon salt
4 tablespoons oil

Soak the rice in water to cover overnight to remove excess starch. The next day, drain and transfer to a heavy-bottomed pot. Add 6 cups water and the salt, and bring to a boil over high heat. Cover the pot and simmer over low heat for 5 minutes. Drain thoroughly.

Pour half the oil into the pot. Rub the oil round the sides of the pot, then add the partially cooked rice. Add the rest of the oil and remaining ½ cup water. Lay a thin kitchen towel or 2 thicknesses of paper toweling over the rice and place the lid on top again, ensuring a firm seal. (Make sure the edges of the towel or paper are well away from the heating element or flame.) Cook the rice on low heat for 20 minutes. Do not lift the lid of the pot or check the rice during this time.

To serve, remove the lid and towel or paper, which should have absorbed excess moisture from the rice. Invert a plate over the pot, and turn the rice out onto it. The rice that was in the bottom of the pan will be crisp and browned. Serve some browned rice to each diner; it is a delicacy.

6

FISH

Sephardic communities have always preferred saltwater fish, but, with the exception of the popular herring, Ashkenazic tradition tends toward freshwater fish. Salted or pickled Baltic and Dutch herring was almost the only source of animal protein for the impoverished Jews of the Pale of Settlement (the area of western Russia and what is now Poland, beyond which Jews were forbidden to live from 1791 until the Revolution). Sephardic Jews who settled in Holland quickly found a taste for the local pickled herrings, and they introduced maatjes herrings and rollmops to the English-speaking countries.

So ingrained is the Ashkenazic habit of eating river fish that even where fish from the sea are cheaper and more plentiful, as in New York and London, carp and pike are preferred. Even the Jews of northern Italy, perhaps under Ashkenazic influence from Austria, prefer to eat trout, carp, and pike on festivals, although they have easy access to good saltwater fish.

Jews in Great Britain and the United States are now showing a preference for saltwater fish. This is probably owing to a combination of availability and freshness, thanks to modern fishing and preserving methods. However the whitefish, native to the Great Lakes, is very popular and can be found in smoked form in every Jewish deli across America.

You will notice that most of these fish dishes can be served hot or cold, and many are more often served cold than hot. This means they are suitable as appetizers as well as entrees, and are very handy for Sabbath meals when cooking is forbidden. If you have not eaten cold fish before, you will be surprised at how good it tastes.

Gefilte Fish

Gefilte fish, or stuffed fish, is the most famous Ashkenazic fish dish. It can be made from any kind of saltwater white fish (cod, scrod, whiting, red snapper, halibut, grouper, yellowtail, etc.), although traditionally freshwater fish such as carp or pike are used. The only unsuitable fish are dark-fleshed oily fish such as herring, mackerel, bonito, and tuna.

The poaching liquid can be any kind of fish court-bouillon. The cooking liquid below is a suggestion, but if you do not have the skin and bones from a fish, use some extra fillets for flavor.

The secret of making great gefilte fish is to poach the fish very gently in liquid that is barely moving. The patties will be light, fluffy, and attractive.

pareve, kosher for Passover

SERVES 6

3 pounds fish, filleted, with trimmings reserved	2 quarts + ¼ cup water
salt and black pepper	pinch of sugar
5 onions, 2 sliced into rings	bunch of fresh parsley
4 carrots	2 stalks celery
2 eggs, lightly beaten	2 slices lemon
3 tablespoons matzo meal	additional cooked carrot slices for garnish

The night before you make the gefilte fish, fillet the fish and place the fillets in a shallow bowl. Salt them lightly. The next day, grind the fish fillets in a food processor along with 3 of the onions and 3 of the carrots. Transfer the mixture to a bowl and add the eggs, matzo meal, ¼ cup water, salt, pepper, and sugar. The mixture should be fluffy and slightly sticky. Set aside.

Put the reserved head, bones, skin, and trimmings from the fish in a large soup pot along with the remaining carrot and onions, the parsley, celery, lemon slices, remaining water, and salt to taste. Bring to a boil and simmer, covered, for 15 minutes over low heat.

Wet your hands and shape the fish mixture into 3-inch patties. Place patties in the simmering broth; add more water to cover the patties, if necessary. Cover pot and simmer fish patties for 1 hour.

Turn off the heat and let the patties cool in the broth. When cool, carefully remove them with a slotted spoon to a serving dish. Strain the broth, then pour it over the patties. Garnish with carrot and onions from the broth. Serve warm or cold, decorated with thin slices of carrot. When served cold, the liquid will jell.

Carpe à la Juive

If Americans associate Jewish cooking with bagels, knishes, and cheese-cake, the French associate it with Carpe à la Juive. Pike can also be used for this dish.

On New Year's, it is traditional to serve the head of the fish to the head of the household. The Hebrew name for the New Year, *Rosh Hashana*, means "Head of the Year," and eating the head is also symbolic of becoming the head, or leader, in righteousness.

pareve

SERVES 6

1 large or 2 small carp, about 2½ pounds	2 cloves garlic, crushed
2 tablespoons oil	1 teaspoon salt
1½ tablespoons all-purpose flour	½ teaspoon black pepper
1 large onion, chopped	1 bay leaf
3 cups water	½ teaspoon dried thyme
	4 tablespoons chopped fresh parsley

Gut and scale the carp. Remove the head and tail and slice it into 1-inch steaks, reserving the head, tail, and any blood.

Heat the oil in a deep pot with a lid over high heat and stir in the flour and 1 tablespoon of the chopped onion. Cook, stirring constantly, for 3 minutes. Add water and bring to a boil, stirring. Add the garlic, remaining onion, salt and pepper, and herbs. Return the liquid to a boil, then add any blood. Put in the fish, including the head and tail. At this point, the liquid will barely cover the fish. Cover the pot and simmer over low heat for 20 minutes.

Carefully remove the pieces of fish from the pot. Arrange on a long platter, forming into the original fish shape. Bring the cooking liquid to a boil over high heat and boil for 5 minutes to reduce somewhat. Strain liquid and pour over fish. Refrigerate the platter; the sauce will jell over the fish. Serve the fish with Chrein (page 184).

Moroccan Fish Balls

This is Moroccan gefilte fish! It is astonishing how very similar recipes spread throughout the Jewish communities of the world, while basic methods remain the same and only the spices and flavors vary according to local taste.

pareve

SERVES 6

1 pound white fish fillets
1 onion, quartered
1 small bunch fresh parsley, coarsely chopped, with stems discarded
1 slice white bread, crust removed
¼ cup water
½ teaspoon salt

½ teaspoon cayenne pepper
½ teaspoon dried marjoram
1 head celery, coarsely chopped, with leaves discarded
1 tablespoon oil
2 cups broth or water

In a food processor or blender, puree the fish with the onion and parsley. Soak the bread in water, then squeeze it dry. Add bread to the fish mixture and season with salt, cayenne pepper, and marjoram. Wet your hands and form ½-inch balls with the fish mixture.

Pour the oil and broth into a deep pot set over high heat. Bring to a boil and add fish balls. Reduce heat and simmer, partially covered, with the water barely moving for 10 minutes.

Add the celery, cover the pot, and simmer for an additional 20 minutes. This dish is a liquid stew or a chunky soup. Serve it hot with rice as an entree.

Pickled Salmon

This is a rather unusual way of cooking salmon that preserves the delicate flavor of this fish. It is a Polish dish, thus more authentic than Scandinavian *gravlaks*, all the rage now at Jewish weddings and bar mitzvahs.

pareve, kosher for Passover

SERVES 4

2½ cups water	1 bay leaf
1 onion, sliced	6 black peppercorns
4 salmon steaks, about 1 inch thick	pinch of brown sugar
½ teaspoon salt	½ cup white vinegar

Bring water to a boil in a saucepan set over high heat. Add the onion and cook for 5 minutes. Add the fish, salt, bay leaf, peppercorns, and brown sugar. Cover and simmer over low heat, with the liquid boiling very gently, for 30 minutes.

Carefully remove the fish with a slotted spoon and lay it in a deep dish, such as a casserole. Stir the vinegar into the cooking liquid, then pour it over the fish. Chill until ready to serve.

Deep-Fried Fish

In his *Point of Arrival,* a history of London's East End, Chaim Bermant quotes a health inspector's report: "There was the Jewish penchant for fried fish, so that at certain times of the week, whole streets were half hidden from view in a mist of frying oil." Fried fish was brought to England by the Sephardic Jews who settled there in the 17th century. It is a dish now firmly entrenched in the Anglo-Jewish tradition, even among the Russian, Polish, German, and Austro-Hungarian Jews who came later. Fried fish is usually accompanied by the horseradish relish called Chrein (page 184).

Fried fish has the advantage of tasting even better cold than hot, so it is exceptionally suitable for Friday night, when cooking is forbidden.

pareve

SERVES 10

3 pounds white saltwater fish, such as halibut, cod, haddock, snapper, or sea bream	3 eggs, lightly beaten
	2 cups matzo meal
	about 3 cups vegetable oil for frying
1 cup all-purpose flour	parsley sprigs for garnish

Wash and trim the fish and cut it into serving portions. Remove bones if desired. Put the flour, eggs, and matzo meal into 3 separate shallow bowls. Have ready plenty of absorbent paper on which to drain the fish.

Heat the oil over high heat in a heavy iron skillet; it should be about 1½ inches deep. It is ready when it smokes very slightly, or until a 1-inch cube of bread dropped into the oil browns in 60 seconds.

While the oil is heating, coat a piece of fish thoroughly with flour, shaking off the excess. Then dip it in the egg and finally in the matzo meal. Place fish in the skillet, and cook, turning with a spatula until brown on both sides, about 8 minutes total. Repeat with several more pieces of fish, but do not fry too many at one time and do not overfill pan. Oil will foam around the fish but should not splatter. As each piece is done, lay it on absorbent paper to drain.

To serve, arrange fish pieces on a large platter. Flat fish look best when placed in a ring, tails meeting in the center and raised slightly. Dot with sprigs of parsley. If served cold, the fish can be cooked a day in advance, and refrigerated.

Turkish Pilaf; recipe on page 67

NOTE

The smell of frying fish is very penetrating. To protect her clothes and hair, my mother would don her "fish-frying regalia," a shower cap and an ancient candlewick bathrobe. The robe has since disintegrated, replaced by an all-enveloping garment that is a combination Moslem chaddor, artist's smock, and flasher's raincoat! She swears I have an aunt in Australia who used to fry fish in a discarded evening dress!

Agristada

Here is another version of fried fish, this time with a lemon sauce, popular in Sephardic communities. As with the previous recipe, the fish can also be served cold.

pareve, kosher for Passover

SERVES 8

2 pounds filleted scrod or whiting, or
   equivalent in halibut steaks
4 tablespoons fine matzo meal
4 tablespoons oil
juice of 2 lemons
4 tablespoons water

½ teaspoon salt
½ teaspoon white pepper
1 teaspoon ground coriander
1 teaspoon ground cumin
3 egg yolks, lightly beaten

Dip the fish pieces in the matzo meal to coat them, then shake off the excess. Heat the oil in a skillet over high heat. Add fish steaks and cook until the flesh is firm, about 5 minutes on each side. Cover skillet and reduce the heat.

Combine the lemon juice with the water, seasonings, and spices. Add this mixture to the skillet and cover again. Cook for 15 minutes.

Remove the skillet from the heat and transfer the fish to a serving platter; keep warm. Pour cooking liquid over the beaten egg yolks, stirring constantly, then return the liquid to the skillet and reheat over low heat until it thickens; do not let it boil. Pour the sauce over the fish and serve.

Fried Gefilte Fish

This is another version of the Cocktail Fish Balls on page 20, but this preparation is much simpler. When molded into long torpedo shapes, the fish is served as an entree. But, however shaped, fried gefilte fish is always eaten cold.

pareve, kosher for Passover

SERVES 4

2 pounds fish fillets
3 onions
2 carrots
4 eggs
1 small potato, grated and drained

½ teaspoon salt
½ teaspoon black pepper
1 cup fine matzo meal
2 cups oil for deep-frying

Put the fish, onions, carrots, 2 of the eggs, the grated potato, salt, and pepper into a food processor. Process until the mixture is well blended and sticks together. Wet your hands and form mixture into torpedo-shaped fingers.

Break the remaining eggs into a shallow bowl and beat well. Pour the matzo meal into another bowl. Heat the oil in a deep-fryer until very hot, about 350°F. Dip the balls in the beaten egg and roll in the matzo meal, then drop in oil. Fry until the coating turns deep golden brown, about 8 minutes. Drain on absorbent paper and let cool. Serve cold.

✡

Baked Whole Fish

I have eaten St. Peter's fish cooked in this way on the shores of the Sea of Galilee. The Sharon Hotel in Herzlia also uses a similar recipe for baking a whole luna fish, a fish too large for the domestic oven but which can be baked whole in the Sharon's catering ovens and served on Saturday evening as part of a buffet.

dairy, kosher for Passover

SERVES 4

4 small trout or fresh whitefish, cleaned
  and dressed
salt and black pepper

juice of ½ lemon
2 onions, sliced
1 cup sour cream

Preheat the oven to 350°F. Place the fish in a greased baking dish and sprinkle with the salt, pepper, and lemon juice. Top with the onion slices, then pour the sour cream over the fish. Bake fish for about 30 minutes, basting every 10 minutes with the pan juices until the fish is golden brown. Serve with salad and baked potatoes.

Curried Fish Fillets

This comes from Cochin in southern India, on the Malabar Coast. At one time there were 2 distinct communities, the "black" and the "white," completely separate from other Indian Jews, most of whom live in Bombay. This fish dish was popular on the Sabbath among the so-called black Jews.

Most of the Cochin Jews now live in Israel. This recipe was given to me by Yvonne Isaac, an old friend from Young Poale Zion, the Zionist youth movement to which I belonged. If you do not like very hot curry, substitute ½ teaspoon chili powder for the whole chili pepper.

pareve, kosher for Passover

SERVES 6

1 tablespoon oil
1 onion, sliced
1½ pounds white fish fillets, cut in
  serving pieces
1 cup water
2 cloves garlic, crushed

small bunch fresh coriander (cilantro)
1 tablespoon herb vinegar
4 tablespoons tomato paste
1 teaspoon ground cumin
½ teaspoon turmeric
1 small red chili pepper (chile pequin)

Heat the oil in a skillet over high heat and sauté the onion until it is transparent, about 5 minutes. Add the fish and sauté until flesh is firm, about 10 minutes. Add the remaining ingredients to the skillet, then cover the pan and simmer over a very low heat so the liquid barely moves for 1 hour. Remove fish pieces to a dish and pour cooking liquid over. Serve with rice.

Halibut Steaks with Fish Liver Dumplings

Fish liver can be bought from good fish merchants, but should be ordered in advance. This is another popular Friday evening entree.

pareve, kosher for Passover

SERVES 6

2 tablespoons oil
2 onions, thinly sliced
6 halibut steaks
1 teaspoon salt
juice of 2 lemons
8 ounces fish liver

3 eggs
2 tablespoons fine matzo meal
1 tablespoon chopped fresh parsley
½ teaspoon black pepper
1 tablespoon cornstarch or potato starch

Heat the oil in a large soup pot set over high heat. Add the onions and sauté until transparent, about 5 minutes. Add the fish steaks and sprinkle with half the salt and the juice of 1 lemon. Cook for 5 minutes, then add enough water to barely cover the fish. Cover the pot and simmer over very low heat for 15 minutes.

While the fish is cooking, bring a saucepan of salted water to a boil over high heat and add the liver. Cook it for 5 minutes, then drain and chop finely, or grind it in a food processor. Add one of the eggs, the matzo meal, parsley, remaining salt, and pepper; mix until smooth. With hands dipped in matzo meal, shape the mixture into dumplings about 1 inch in diameter. Add the dumplings to the fish and cook, covered, at a bare simmer, for 15 minutes.

Carefully remove the fish and dumplings from the pot. Arrange the fish in the center of a serving platter and garnish with the dumplings.

Strain the liquid in which the fish was cooked. Combine the cornstarch with the juice of the remaining lemon, then add 2 cups of the cooking liquid. (If there is not enough liquid to make 2 cups, add water.) Pour the liquid into a saucepan and bring it to a boil over high heat, stirring constantly. Cook for 3 minutes, then remove the pot from the heat.

Beat the 2 remaining eggs, then gradually add some of the cooking liquid, beating constantly to prevent curdling. Return liquid to the pot, set over low heat, and stir constantly until sauce thickens; do not let it boil, or sauce will curdle. Pour the sauce over the fish. Serve warm or cold.

Waterzooie

A recipe for this Dutch fish stew appears in the first English-language Jewish cookbook under the anglicized name "water souchy." Photo opposite page 77.

dairy

SERVES 6

2 parsnips, sliced
3 white or yellow onions, quartered
3 cups water
juice and rind of 1 lemon
1 teaspoon wine vinegar
⅛ teaspoon saffron strands
pinch of grated nutmeg or mace
1 bay leaf

1 teaspoon salt
½ teaspoon white pepper
4 large white fish fillets, about
  2½ pounds
1 tablespoon all-purpose flour
1 tablespoon butter, softened
1 egg yolk

Put the parsnips and onions in a saucepan over high heat and add water. Cover the pan and bring to a boil. Cook for 15 minutes, or until the parsnips and onions are soft. Add the lemon juice and rind, vinegar, spices and herbs, and salt and pepper. Simmer over low heat for 5 minutes, then add the fish and simmer, covered, for 15 minutes.

Remove the fish carefully and reserve it. Strain the cooking liquid. In a small bowl, with a spoon work the flour and butter together into a paste. Stir paste into the cooking liquid and stir to dissolve. Beat in the egg yolk, then return the liquid to the stove and stir over low heat until it thickens. If the dish is to be served hot, return the fish to the pan to reheat. If served cold, pour the liquid over the fish and let cool, then refrigerate until required. Garnish with parsley sprigs and lemon slices.

7

MEAT AND POULTRY ENTREES

Traditional Jewish meat dishes are usually slow-cooked. The koshering process and the fact that meat may not be allowed to hang, and thus become tender, makes this the most suitable cooking method. It is also the most easily digestible way of cooking meat, as it breaks down the fibers to permit maximum absorption of the nutrients.

Whatever method is used, Jews everywhere prefer well-cooked meat. Kosher butchers confirm what I have heard from many Orthodox Jewish women, namely that the Jewish housewife assumes that the fresher the meat and more recently killed, the better it will be, and that any sign of redness or ink juices in cooked meat is distasteful.

Ashkenazi Jews prefer beef, since lamb and mutton are virtually unknown in Eastern Europe. Among Sephardic, Middle Eastern, and North African Jews, however, lamb is the favorite as well as the most easily available meat. It is, of course, traditional on Passover.

Poultry is also very popular. Nowadays, that means mostly chicken and turkey. Goose was the most important meat in Central and Eastern Europe, as well as in northern Italy, where Jewish goose salami is still a great delicacy among non-Jews as well. Today goose is a luxury, but efficient poultry-rearing methods have ensured a kosher chicken in every Jewish pot.

Slow-Cooked Sabbath Stew

There are almost as many recipes for this kind of stew—or cholent—as there are Askenazi Jewish families. The idea is to use slow-cooking ingredients, such as tougher cuts of meat and dried beans, and to simmer the stew for as long as possible. If the oven has been used just before Friday night to bake something like a potato pudding, which needs high heat, the stew gets a good quick start. In fact, anything cooked overnight for the Sabbath should be one-third cooked before the Sabbath starts.

Edouard de Pomiane, the famous French food writer and broadcaster, studied Jewish cuisine in Poland. He claimed cholent is not so much a recipe, but a cooking technique that can be used with a variety of ingredients. Cholent, known among German Jews as shalet, is the Ashkenazic word for stew, apparently derived from the French *chaudlent*, meaning "hot-slow."

meat

can be slow-cooked for Sabbath

SERVES 8

1 cup dried lima, navy, or great northern beans	½ teaspoon paprika
3 tablespoons chicken fat or vegetable shortening	¼ teaspoon ground ginger
	1 cup barley
3 large onions, sliced	2 pounds potatoes, peeled
3 pounds boneless flank or brisket	2 cloves garlic
1 teaspoon dried thyme	salt and black pepper

Soak the beans overnight in water to cover. Drain and discard the soaking water.

Heat the fat in a heavy casserole over high heat and sweat the onions, covered with a tight-fitting lid, until soft and browned, about 15 minutes. Remove onions with a slotted spoon and set aside.

Sprinkle the meat with the herbs and spices. Add to casserole and brown it all over in the hot fat, turning frequently. Add the remaining ingredients, then enough boiling water to cover. Cover the casserole tightly and bring ingredients to a boil.

Preheat the oven to 400°F. Once liquid has come to a boil, put the casserole in the oven and cook for 30 minutes. Then reduce the heat to the lowest setting (about 250°F), and simmer overnight and until noon the next day. Do not stir. When ready to serve, remove casserole from the oven and season with salt and pepper to taste. Serve hot.

A kugel (see page 98) is often cooked in a well-sealed pudding basin inside the cholent pot. Alternately, serve with Kishka (page 65), Stuffed Neck (page 66), or Potato Dumpling (page 58).

Dfina

Dfina is a Sephardic version of the slow-cooked stew. It is prepared all over the Middle East as well as in Turkey and Spain. This version is from Egypt, distinguished by the hard-cooked eggs with their delicious, creamy yolks. The dried white beans are such a standard ingredient in these Sabbath stews that the Spanish name for them is *judías*, meaning "Jews." Greek Jews call the beans *fijones*, and their version of this stew is *fijonicas*.

meat

can be slow-cooked for Sabbath

SERVES 8

8 ounces chick peas (garbanzo beans)	6 small potatoes, peeled
8 ounces navy beans	6 eggs in their shells
2 tablespoons oil	4 cloves garlic, minced
2 large onions, finely chopped	1 teaspoon ground coriander
2 pounds boneless beef (flank steak or	1 teaspoon ground cumin seed
brisket), cut into chunks or pieces, fat	1 teaspoon ground allspice
trimmed	salt and black pepper

Soak the beans and chick peas overnight in water to cover. Drain and discard soaking water.

Heat the oil in a skillet and sauté the chopped onions until golden brown, about 5 minutes.

Put the meat, potatoes, onions, and whole eggs in their shells into a large ovenproof pot or casserole with a tight-fitting lid. Add beans and chick peas to the pot. Then add the garlic and spices, but not the salt and pepper.

Preheat the oven to 375°F. Add enough water to the pot to barely cover the ingredients. If the lid of the pot does not fit tightly, put a layer of foil between the pot and lid.

Bake the stew for 1 hour, then add the salt and pepper, and reduce the heat to the lowest setting in the oven, about 250°F. Cook for at least 5 hours or overnight. Serve at lunch next day, with Sephardic Sabbath Rice (page 68).

Cholent-Style Liver

For this recipe, use one piece of liver, cut into an oblong or square.

meat, kosher for Passover
can be slow-cooked for Sabbath

SERVES 8

3 tablespoons chicken fat	*2 onions, sliced*
2 pounds koshered beef or calves' liver	*½ teaspoon salt*
2 cups water	*½ teaspoon paprika*
2 carrots, sliced	

Heat the fat in a skillet over high heat and the liver until it is evenly coated. Put the meat into a casserole or Dutch oven and add the rest of the ingredients. Cover the pot and bring to a boil.

Preheat the oven to 325°F. When liquid boils, transfer the casserole to the oven and cook for 2 hours. Then reduce the heat to minimum, about 250°F, and simmer for 8 hours or overnight. Serve with Farfel (page 52) or a kugel (pages 54, 61).

Jewish-Style Pot Roast

This is just one version of sweet-and-sour pot roast, typical of German and Austrian Jewish cooking. Photo opposite page 61.

meat

SERVES 6 TO 8

3 pounds boneless beef (brisket or boned and rolled shoulder)	boiling water
	1 slice stale rye bread, crust removed
6 large onions, quartered	½ cup honey
1 teaspoon dried thyme	juice of 1 lemon
1 bay leaf	salt and black pepper

Place the meat in a large, heavy pot or casserole and add onions, thyme, and bay leaf. Add enough boiling water to cover the meat. Place pot over high heat and bring the water to a boil. Then reduce the heat and cover the pot. Simmer the meat for 2½ hours, checking to see that the water is not completely absorbed and adding more boiling water as necessary.

Pour a couple tablespoons of boiling water over the bread to soften it and mash it with a fork. Add this mixture to the meat. Then add the honey, 2 more cups boiling water, and the lemon juice. Cook, uncovered, turning frequently, until the meat is browned, about 20 minutes. Add salt and pepper to taste, and serve.

Prune Tsimmes

Combinations of dried fruits and meats are typical of Middle Eastern cooking. It is likely this recipe was introduced into Europe during the Middle Ages by Jewish traders from the Middle East, or by Sephardic Jews fleeing the Inquisition. Cook it in stages, and let the meat cool completely before slicing.

meat, kosher for Passover

SERVES 4

2 tablespoons chicken fat or shortening
2 pounds boneless beef brisket
1 quart water
1 cup Farfel or Matzo Farfel (pages
   52-53)
1 cup pitted prunes

½ teaspoon salt
⅛ teaspoon ground cinnamon
⅛ teaspoon grated nutmeg
1 small onion, grated
¼ cup honey
juice and grated rind of 1 lemon

Melt the fat in a Dutch oven or casserole, then brown the meat evenly over high heat. Drain off fat and add water. Bring the water to a boil, skimming off the scum which rises to the surface.

Add the farfel to the boiling liquid gradually, stirring to prevent sticking. Cover pot and simmer over low heat for 30 minutes.

Add the remaining ingredients to the pot, stir, and cover. Simmer for an additional 1 hour.

Preheat oven to 350°F. Remove the meat from broth and let cool. Pour the cooking liquid into a baking dish. Slice the meat evenly and arrange it over the liquid, then bake for 30 minutes, basting halfway through with the pan juices. Serve with rice, barley, or kasha.

Stuffed Cabbage Rolls

Stuffed vegetables are a traditional way of stretching a meager meat ration, and are especially useful in Jewish cooking because the meat can be either precooked or raw. Stuffed cabbage rolls are popular among all Ashkenazic communities, but especially in Poland and western Russia. They have many names—*holishkes* and *golubtsy* are just 2 of them.

There are many variations on this recipe, and whichever I use, someone will tell me it isn't the authentic one! This version is for Judy Jeanson's father. Judy Jeanson runs a catering establishment in West Los Angeles. Her father helped her set up her business and, unusual for a Jewish man, he has a hand in the kitchen as well. Stuffed cabbage rolls are his specialty, and I hope these taste something like the delicious ones he makes. Sour salt—citric acid crystals—available in the Jewish section of most supermarkets. It is very strong, so use it sparingly. Photo opposite page 60.

meat

SERVES 4

8 large whole cabbage leaves	½ cup uncooked rice
1 pound ground beef	2 cups canned tomatoes, with juice
salt and black pepper	1 tablespoon paprika
1 onion, grated	⅛ teaspoon sour salt
1 clove garlic, minced	2 tablespoons brown sugar
1 tablespoon golden raisins	

Make sure the cabbage leaves you use are free of blemishes, holes, or tears. Plunge them into boiling water for 3 minutes to soften the veins so they can be rolled up.

Season the meat with salt and pepper, then mix it well with the onion, garlic, raisins, and rice. Arrange the cabbage leaves on a flat surface. Place 2 tablespoons of filling in the center of each cabbage leaf. Fold the sides of the leaves to the center, then roll the cabbage leaf up toward you, to firmly enclose the stuffing. Tie the cabbage packages with strong thread.

Put the remaining ingredients in a shallow pan with a lid. Bring to a boil over high heat, stirring occasionally. Arrange the cabbage packages in the pan and cover. Reduce heat and simmer at a low boil for 1 hour, or until the leaves are tender and the contents cooked. Baste the cabbage packages with the sauce every 20 minutes, and add a little water if too much liquid evaporates. Serve hot.

Albóndigas

Meatballs, large and small, are a Jewish staple. The Sephardic name for meatballs is *albóndigas*, and this is one version of that dish. With different seasonings and larger meatballs, you will have the Ashkenazic dish baked klops.

Meatballs are always half meat, half starch, so they are extremely economical. The starch is either soaked bread or rice. You must, of course, use nondairy white bread.

meat

SERVES 4

1 slice white bread, crust removed	*1 egg*
2 cups meat or vegetable broth	*2 tablespoons margarine*
8 ounces chopped or ground beef or lamb	*2 tablespoons all-purpose flour*
salt and black pepper	*juice and grated rind of 1 lemon*
2 cloves garlic, minced	*4 tablespoons chopped fresh parsley*
½ teaspoon ground cinnamon	

Soak the bread in the broth and squeeze it to expel excess moisture. In a bowl, combine bread with the meat, seasonings, garlic, and cinnamon. Bind mixture with the egg, then shape into meatballs the size of walnuts.

Melt the margarine in a skillet and stir in the flour; blend well. Cook for 2 minutes over high heat, then add the broth, stirring constantly, and bring to a boil.

Add the lemon juice and parsley and cook for 2 minutes. Drop the meatballs into the broth and reduce heat. Simmer, covered, until meatballs are cooked, about 30 minutes. Serve meatballs and sauce with rice.

Siniyeh

This Yemenite dish is similar to the Greek dish moussaka, but it uses tahina (sesame seed paste) instead of cheese to achieve a similar effect but remain kosher. You can either make your own tahina or buy it canned.

meat

SERVES 4

2 pounds lean ground lamb or beef
2 tablespoons chopped fresh parsley
2 onions, minced
2 cloves garlic, crushed
½ teaspoon ground cinnamon

salt and black pepper
¼ cup olive oil
2 tablespoons pine nuts (pignoli)
1 cup Tahina (page 18)

In a large bowl, mix the ground meat with the parsley, onions, garlic, and cinnamon. Chop the mixture again or puree it in a food processor. Season with salt and black pepper.

Preheat the oven to 400°F. Oil a shallow 2-quart baking dish and spread it evenly with the meat mixture. Heat 1 tablespoon of the oil in a skillet and fry the pine nuts, stirring constantly, until they are lightly browned, about 5 minutes. Remove pine nuts from the heat immediately and sprinkle them and the oil in which they were cooked over the meat mixture.

Bake the dish for 10 minutes or until browned on top. Pour the tahina evenly over the mixture and bake another 15 minutes, or until browned and bubbling. Serve with rice and salad.

Tunisian-Style Couscous

Couscous is the national dish of Tunisia, although it is also popular in Morocco and Algeria. In all these countries, couscous is the traditional Friday-night Jewish dinner.

Couscous is coarse farina, rolled and rubbed with a little liquid until the grains swell. It used to be common in the development towns of Israel to see North African women sitting in front of their houses, with large metal bowls between their knees. They would be rubbing and rolling the couscous; when it was ready, they would store it for future use. Nowadays, you can buy ready-made couscous, which can be cooked faster.

Couscous is cooked over the steam produced by a delicious stew. The grains are flavored with the steam, and are served along with the liquid. The secret of a good couscous is to use turnips in the cooking liquid.

Couscous is made in a special pot—a *couscousier*—which can be bought in Middle Eastern shops. If you do not have one, place a vegetable steamer over a heavy saucepan. The great thing about couscous is that it is one huge meal in itself, and doesn't need side dishes or accompaniments. There always seems to be enough even to feed unexpected guests.

The hot sauce *harissa* is available in small cans from Middle Eastern stores, but if you can't get it, combine 1 teaspoon Tabasco with ½ cup tomato sauce. Another favorite couscous ingredient is the spicy sausage known as *merguez*. A good substitute is Mexican-style *chorizo*. Photo opposite.

meat

SERVES 8

2 cups chick peas	2 carrots, split lengthwise
2 tablespoons oil	2 bell peppers, seeded and sliced
2 pounds boneless neck or shoulder of lamb, cubed	1 teaspoon ground ginger
	2 teaspoons ground coriander
1 onion, finely chopped	1 teaspoon cayenne pepper
1 marrow bone	½ teaspoon ground cumin
4 medium tomatoes, peeled and chopped	pinch of saffron
2 cloves garlic, crushed	1 teaspoon harissa (see recipe introduction)
4 small or 2 large turnips, quartered	
2 zucchini, sliced	2 quarts water
1 cup cubed pumpkin or squash	

Soak the chick peas overnight in water to cover. Drain and rinse. Heat the oil in a large saucepan over high heat and brown the meat and onion until the meat is colored and the onion is transparent. Add the marrow bone and drained chick peas. Reduce heat, cover, and cook until meat is tender, about 2 hours.

While meat cooks, prepare vegetables and couscous. Put the vegetables and spices into the bottom half of a steamer or couscous pot and add water. Place over high heat, cover the pot, and while the mixture is coming to a

Tunisian-Style Couscous

boil, rinse the couscous in cold water. Spread it out on a tray and rub it to separate the grains. Set aside for 10 minutes.

Transfer the couscous to the top half of the pot or steamer. Reduce heat to low. Cover the pot and seal the 2 halves together with a strip of damp cheesecloth. Simmer for 30 minutes.

Remove the couscous from the pot and transfer it to a tray. Sprinkle it with cold water and run a fork through it to separate the grains. Return it to the pot, cover and seal it, and cook for another 30 minutes.

To serve, add the meat and chick peas to the vegetable stew; stir to blend well. Pile the couscous in a mound on a large dish. Arrange some of the stew around and on top of the couscous. Pour on just enough broth to be absorbed by the couscous. Serve remaining broth and stew on the side, with extra harissa for those who like even more spicy couscous.

Kurdish Kibbeh

Kibbeh is another kind of meatball, cooked inside a shell of cracked wheat or bulgur, partially cooked cracked wheat. Kibbeh is eaten in Lebanon, Syria, Iraq, and Kurdistan. What makes the Kurdish version different is pomegranate seeds. They add an interesting sour note and an attractive reddish-brown color to the stew. Pomegranates are in season only in the fall; when not in season, replace with ½ cup pine nuts (pignolis). Photo opposite.

meat

SERVES 4

1 pound lean ground lamb
1 cup bulgur
1 cup semolina
½ teaspoon ground cumin
4 ounces koshered lamb's liver

2 cups oil
2 onions, chopped
½ cup raisins
1 cup pomegranate seeds

To make the kibbeh shells, place 4 ounces of the meat in a blender or food processor and process until it is a paste. Set aside.

Rinse the bulgur in cold water and squeeze it dry. Place bulgur in a blender or food processor and add the meat paste and the semolina. Process until the mixture resembles a firm dough. If it does not adhere well, add a few drops of water. Transfer mixture to a bowl and chill for 1 hour while you make the filling.

Puree the remaining meat with the liver in a blender or food processor. Heat 2 tablespoons of the oil in a skillet over high heat and cook the onions until transparent, about 3 or 4 minutes. Add the raisins and meat, and cook until lightly browned, stirring constantly. Remove from the heat and stir in the pomegranate seeds.

To assemble the kibbeh, knead the dough for 5 minutes. Take a walnut-size piece of the dough and shape it into a ball. Flatten the ball and poke your finger into it, gradually hollowing out a cavity and shaping the dough into a torpedo shape. Fill the cavity with about a tablespoon of the stuffing mixture and work the dough over the hole to close it. Continue to assemble the kibbeh. When all have been assembled, arrange on a dish and chill for 1 hour.

Heat the remainder of the oil in a deep-fryer until it registers 375°F on a thermometer or a cube of bread browns in 60 seconds. Drop in the kibbeh, a few at a time. Deep-fry until golden-brown, about 10 minutes, then drain on absorbent paper. Keep warm as you continue to cook kibbeh. Serve with saffron or white rice, perhaps accompanied by sautéed peppers.

Passover Tongue with Sweet-and-Sour Sauce

This is another classic Polish dish, adapted here for Passover. At other times of the year, cookies made with honey and black pepper would be crumbled into the sauce instead of matzo meal and pepper seasoning.

meat, kosher for Passover

SERVES 4

1 pickled ox tongue or 4 lamb's tongues	1½ cups beef broth or consommé
1 tablespoon margarine	¼ cup wine vinegar
1 onion, chopped	2 tablespoons brown sugar
2 tablespoons matzo meal	2 tablespoons golden raisins
juice of 1 lemon	1 teaspoon black pepper

Place tongue in a pot with cold water to cover. Bring to a boil over high heat, then reduce heat and simmer, with the water barely moving, for 2 hours.

Drain tongue. Peel and slice thinly, then arrange in overlapping slices on a serving platter. Keep warm.

Melt the margarine in a saucepan set over high heat. Add the onion and cook until transparent but not browned, about 5 minutes. Stir in the matzo meal, and when the mixture is smooth, add the lemon juice and beef broth or consommé. Stir until smooth. Reduce heat, cover the pot, and simmer for 5 minutes.

In another saucepan, heat the vinegar. Stir in the brown sugar and cook over high heat, stirring until the liquid thickens and becomes syrupy, about 10 minutes. Stir vinegar mixture into the broth mixture, then add the raisins and season with pepper. Pour sauce over the tongue, and serve.

Veal Rolls for the Sabbath

This recipe is from Mantua in Italy. Veal is, of course, a favorite Italian meat. It is rather an unusual recipe. Photo opposite page 108.

meat

SERVES 4

3 tablespoons oil	salt and black pepper
4 eggs	1 teaspoon dried sage
1 cup cooked peas	1 cup water
4 lean veal cutlets	bone marrow (optional)

Heat ½ tablespoon of the oil in a small skillet. In a bowl, lightly beat 1 egg and stir in ¼ cup of peas. Pour the mixture into the skillet and cook over medium heat for 3 minutes on one side, 1 minute on the other. Remove and drain on absorbent paper. Repeat with the remaining eggs and peas, oiling the pan as required, and making 3 more omelets.

Sandwich the veal cutlets between sheets of waxed paper and flatten with a steak hammer. Remove waxed paper and lay a piece of veal on top of each omelet. Season with salt and pepper and roll up each omelet so that the cutlet is encased in the omelet.

Heat the remaining oil with the sage in a saucepan with a lid, and add the veal rolls. Add water, set over low heat, and cover the pan. If desired, add a few pieces of bone marrow to the cooking liquid. Simmer for 1 hour, or until the veal is firm but tender.

Remove pan from the heat and let contents cool. When the rolls are cold, slice into strips, and serve cold with the sauce.

Chicken Stuffed with Orange

This is another Israeli favorite for festive occasions and Friday nights.

meat, kosher for Passover

SERVES 4

1 lemon
2½- to 3-pound chicken
2 oranges
2 teaspoons salt
2 cloves garlic, minced

2 teaspoons paprika
1 teaspoon chili powder
1 teaspoon ground coriander
1 cup water
2 onions

Preheat oven to 425°F. Cut the lemon in half and rub one half over the chicken. Then squeeze the juice into a bowl, as well as the juice from one of the oranges.

Put the chicken in a roasting pan. Mix the salt, garlic, and spices together in a small bowl, then sprinkle them over the chicken inside and out. Stuff chicken with the remaining orange. Pour the lemon and orange juices into the pan around chicken and add water. Cut the onions in half and add them to the pan.

Cook the chicken for 15 minutes, then baste with pan juices and lower the heat to 350°F. Roast for 1 hour, basting after 30 minutes.

Let chicken rest for 10 minutes, then transfer to serving dish. Cut the whole orange and the halved onions into pieces and serve with the chicken. This is delicious with rice or pasta.

Georgian Chicken with Grapes

There are so many immigrants from the Soviet Republic of Georgia now in Israel that this dish has entered the Israeli repertoire. The Georgian climate is similar to that of the Mediterranean, and Georgian wines are the best in the U.S.S.R. This dish is served on Friday nights. Instead of pot-roasting the chicken, you can also oven roast it.

meat, kosher for Passover

SERVES 4 TO 6

1 lemon
1 whole roasting or frying chicken, about
   3 pounds
3 tablespoons oil
3 onions, chopped
2 cups ground beef or lamb
½ teaspoon black pepper
½ teaspoon ground cinnamon
¼ teaspoon grated nutmeg

¼ teaspoon ground cloves
½ teaspoon salt
about 2 cups unsweetened red grape
   juice
1 teaspoon sugar
½ cup water
2 tablespoons blanched almonds, halved
small grape clusters for garnish

Squeeze the juice from the lemon and reserve. Rub the empty lemon halves over the chicken.

Heat the oil in a large, deep skillet over high heat and fry the onions until transparent, about 5 minutes. Add the onions and ground beef or lamb and sauté, stirring frequently, until the meat loses its redness. Drain off the excess fat and reserve it. Sauté meat another 5 minutes, then add the spices, salt, 1 cup grape juice, lemon juice, and sugar to the pan. Cook, stirring frequently, until most of the liquid has evaporated, about 7 minutes. Stuff the chicken with the meat mixture.

Pour the reserved fat back into the skillet and brown the chicken all over. Transfer chicken to Dutch oven or casserole and add ½ cup grape juice, water, and the almonds to the pot. Cover tightly and simmer over very low heat for 3 hours, or until cooked through. Baste every 30 minutes with pan juices and add more grape juice if liquid diminishes. Transfer chicken to a serving platter and pour cooking liquid over. Decorate with grape clusters before serving. Serve with white rice.

Chicken with Egg-and-Lemon Sauce

This is a Passover favorite in my family. Use a boiling fowl if possible, the largest roasting chicken you can find, or even a small turkey.

meat, kosher for Passover

SERVES 6 TO 8

1 chicken, 4 to 6 pounds	1 small bunch fresh parsley
1 teaspoon salt	2 lemons
2 turnips, quartered	1 tablespoon potato starch
2 onions, 1 stuck with 2 whole cloves	2 egg yolks, lightly beaten
1 clove garlic	pinch of black pepper
2 stalks celery	pinch of grated nutmeg

Remove as much fat from chicken as possible (some people also like to pull off as much skin as they can; this reduces the fat content of the broth). Put the chicken in a deep soup pot. Add water to barely cover it, and sprinkle in the salt. Bring the water rapidly to a boil over high heat. Skim off the foam on the surface of the water, then add the turnips, onions, garlic, celery, and parsley. Reduce the heat to low and cover the pot. Simmer the chicken for 1½ hours, or until tender.

Remove the chicken from the pot and cut into serving pieces. Keep warm on a serving platter. Strain the broth, then let cool to room temperature. Use a paper towel to skim as much fat from the surface of the broth as possible. Reheat broth over high heat and then boil it, uncovered, for 15 minutes to reduce somewhat.

Grate the lemon rind and add the grated peel to the broth. Squeeze the lemon juice and mix well with the cornstarch. Remove broth from the heat and add potato starch mixture, stirring until smooth. Pour the thickened cooking liquid into the top part of a double boiler, and place over hot water. Keep double boiler on a low heat and, stirring constantly, add the beaten egg yolks to the broth. Stir constantly until the sauce thickens.

Serve the chicken with a little of the sauce poured over; have more sauce on the side.

Hamin

Hamin is the Hebrew word for cholent, and it derives from the word *ham* for "hot." Some Sephardic communities use this word, as do the Persian and Italian Jews. There are also many versions of hamin; this is an Afghan recipe.

The Jews of Afghanistan have a very economical way of cooking for the Sabbath. This chicken stew is cooked in the bottom of a double earthenware pot; the top part contains fish with tomatoes. You can cook 2 meals at the same time, and the fish is served on Friday night while the stew is offered at midday on Saturday. Use the same technique with a large double boiler or 2-level steamer, covering the holes with foil.

Quinces are large yellow fruits which look like apples but have a much tougher and more sour flesh. The flesh turns an attractive pink when cooked, and is delicious with meat or chicken, or stewed with sugar and cloves as a dessert. Quinces figure prominently in Persian, Afghan, and Kurdish cooking. Dried rosebuds are available from Middle Eastern shops.

meat, can be slow-cooked for Sabbath

SERVES 8

4 tablespoons oil

2 chickens, about 3 pounds each, cut in
   serving pieces

2 potatoes, sliced

2 carrots, sliced

1 pound pumpkin or squash, peeled and
   cut into chunks

2 cups uncooked long-grain rice

2 large quinces (about 1 pound weight),
   peeled, cored, and quartered

2 onions, sliced

1 teaspoon ground cinnamon

1/2 teaspoon salt

1/2 teaspoon black pepper

1 tablespoon rosebuds or petals
   (optional)

2 eggs, lightly beaten

6 cups water

Pour half the oil into a large skillet set over medium heat. Add the chicken and cook evenly until the flesh is no longer transparent, about 15 minutes. Remove and reserve the chicken. Preheat oven to 425°F. Pour any oil remaining in the skillet plus the remaining 2 tablespoons of oil into a large casserole with a tight-fitting lid. Add a layer of sliced potatoes, carrots, and squash to cover the bottom of the pan. Lay the rice on top.

Arrange the chicken pieces over rice and place the onion slices and quince pieces around and over chicken. Sprinkle with the spices, seasonings, and rosebuds or petals. Beat the eggs with the water and pour over the contents of the casserole.

Bake chicken for 20 minutes, then reduce the heat to 250°F and bake for 8 hours or overnight. Serve with rice at lunch the next day.

Indian Stewed Chicken

The Beni Israel of Bombay usually serve this chicken with the deep-fried potatoes known as Aloo Makalla (page 114), though it is equally delicious with rice. Garam masala is a curry mix that can be found in the international section of many supermarkets, but if you can't find it, substitute a good curry powder. Instead of cooking it at 250°F, you can stew this chicken overnight cholent-style in a tightly covered pot.

meat, kosher for Passover
can be slow-cooked for Sabbath

SERVES 4

½ cup oil
1 chicken, about 3 pounds, cut in
   serving pieces
1 onion, thinly sliced
1 cinnamon stick
4 cloves
4 cardamom pods

2 bay leaves
1 tablespoon garam masala
1 tablespoon grated ginger root
2 cloves garlic, minced
¼ teaspoon turmeric
1 cup chicken broth (optional)

Preheat oven to 250°F. Heat the oil in a flameproof casserole with a tight-fitting lid. When hot, add the chicken, onion, and remaining ingredients. Cook, stirring and turning frequently, until the chicken flesh loses its transparency, about 15 minutes.

Cover the casserole and bake for at least 1½ hours, stirring and basting every 20 minutes. If all the oil is absorbed before the end of the cooking time and the chicken begins looking dry, add some of the chicken broth. Remove the lid and let chicken brown for 10 minutes before serving.

Chicken with Olives

This is the dish on which Moroccan Jews break their fast after the Day of Atonement. Use imported green olives, which are flavored with cayenne pepper and garlic, available in Middle Eastern stores. Canned, pitted olives can be substituted, but they have less flavor. Photo opposite page 109.

meat, kosher for Passover

SERVES 4 TO 6

*1 large chicken, about 3½ pounds, cut
  in serving pieces
2 cloves garlic
salt and black pepper
½ teaspoon cayenne pepper
½ teaspoon paprika*

*½ teaspoon ground coriander
pinch of saffron
2 tablespoons oil
2 pounds green olives
2 Pickled Lemons (page 178), or fresh
  lemons, sliced*

Rub the chicken with the garlic and sprinkle with the spices. Heat the oil in a deep saucepan over medium heat and add the chicken pieces. Add enough water to barely cover the chicken. Bring to a boil, then reduce heat and simmer, covered, for 1½ hours.

Meanwhile, pit and rinse the olives. Add olives and lemon slices to the chicken and cook over very low heat for an additional hour. Remove chicken from pot and serve with boiled rice, pouring the broth from the pan over the rice to make a sauce.

✡

Chicken-Stuffed Quinces

This is a very delicate Persian dish for Sabbath Eve. Rosewater is available in specialty groceries and Middle Eastern shops.

meat

SERVES 6

*6 large quinces
juice of 1 lemon
2 chicken breasts, boned
3 tablespoons matzo meal
¼ teaspoon ground cloves*

*½ teaspoon ground cinnamon
½ teaspoon rosewater
¼ teaspoon salt
2 tablespoons margarine, cut in pieces
about 1 cup water or chicken broth*

Parboil the whole quinces in water to cover for 10 minutes; this will make them easier to prepare, as they are very woody in texture. Peel quinces and slice in half lengthwise. Scoop out the core and most of the flesh Sprinkle shells with the lemon juice to stop discoloration.

Preheat oven to 400°F.

Puree the chicken breasts in a food processor or blender with the matzo meal and spices, rosewater, and salt. Fill the quince shells with the mixture, packing it tightly and shaping into a mound. Dot each with a piece of margarine. Place quinces in a baking dish and pour in water or chicken broth to come ½ inch up the sides.

Bake for 1 hour, or until the quinces are soft and the meat is cooked through. Serve hot with a rice dish (see pages 67–69).

Barbecued Chicken Hearts

Barbecued meats are popular in the Middle East, though they are not marinated or brushed with sauce in the American tradition. I first tasted these at a tiny booth in Jerusalem, where an old Yemenite broiled the chicken hearts over charcoal. Chicken hearts are very inexpensive and very delicious—this recipe is simplicity itself.

meat

SERVES 8

1 pound, about 2 cups, koshered chicken hearts	Israeli Salad (recipe page 117)
8 pita breads	salt
	Tabasco or other hot sauce

Thread the chicken hearts onto 8 long skewers, allowing 6 hearts per skewer. Broil the hearts over a charcoal grill or under a broiler, turning frequently to ensure even cooking. When they start to brown, after about 7 minutes, they are done.

Cut each pita bread across the top and put 1 tablespoon of salad inside. Add hearts from 1 skewer and sprinkle with salt and a few drops of hot sauce. Serve immediately.

Turkey Schnitzel

This is a favorite Israeli dish, based loosely on its Viennese counterpart but reflecting both a Middle Eastern influence and an Israeli individuality.

meat

SERVES 4

2 turkey breasts, about 1 pound	*½ cup all-purpose flour*
salt and black pepper	*½ cup matzo meal*
1 teaspoon minced onion	*1 cup oil for frying*
1 teaspoon ground cumin	*lemon slices*
2 eggs	*parsley sprigs*
2 tablespoons water	

Remove any skin and bones from the turkey breasts and cut the meat into slices about ¾ inch thick (or have the butcher do this for you). Place each slice between 2 pieces of waxed paper and flatten with a steak hammer. Remove the waxed paper and sprinkle meat on both sides with the salt, pepper, and spices.

Beat the eggs with the water and pour the mixture into a shallow dish. Put the flour into another shallow dish and the matzo meal into a third shallow dish. Heat the oil in a skillet over high heat. Dip a slice of turkey into the egg mixture, coating it thoroughly. Then dip it lightly in the flour and finally in the matzo meal. The slices should be completely covered with batter on both sides.

Fry until brown and crisp on both sides, about 10 minutes. Garnish with slices of lemon and sprigs of parsley. Serve hot with mashed potatoes or french fries.

Goose with Apples

Goose once occupied the central place in the Jewish diet that chicken does today. In Central and Eastern Europe, goose fat was the universal cooking medium, while the tough flesh was ideal for cooking overnight in a cholent. The famous French cassoulet—preserved goose with beans—is almost certainly of Jewish origin, since records of the Inquisition in Carcassonne show that victims were accused of Jewish tendencies if they made these slow-cooked goose stews.

Today goose is less frequently served, but still available. The following is a good way to cook goose, because the slow cooking gently tenderizes the toughest bird. Serve with Roast Potatoes with Rice (page 113) or, at Passover, with Matzo Farfel (page 53), and Sweet-and-Sour Red Cabbage (page 112).

meat, kosher for Passover

SERVES 6 TO 8

1 young goose, about 5 pounds, cut in 8 serving pieces	8 green apples, peeled, cored, and quartered
2 tablespoons rendered goose fat	1 teaspoon paprika
½ teaspoon salt	1 cup water
2 onions, finely chopped	

Remove as much fat as possible from the bird. Render some and use as the cooking medium.

Heat the goose fat in a casserole or Dutch oven set over high heat and evenly brown the pieces of goose for 10 minutes. Sprinkle with salt. Remove goose and add the onions, frying them to a golden color, about 5 minutes. Add the apples and sprinkle with paprika. Add water, cover pot, and simmer over low heat for 3 hours or until meat is tender. Check every 15 minutes and add more water if necessary to keep goose moist. At the end of the cooking time there should be no liquid left in the pan, however, and apples should have cooked in the goose fat. Serve immediately.

8

VEGETABLES

Vegetables have always played an important part in the Jewish diet. Like fish, they are neither meat nor milk, so they can be eaten with every meal. Root vegetables are abundant and cheap, thus always a major food in poor Jewish communities. An old Yiddish song goes, "Potatoes on Monday, potatoes on Tuesday. . . ."

There has always been a flourishing vegetarian movement among European Jews. In Israel, red meat is very expensive and generally of poor quality, so many people have stopped eating it altogether. Subsequently, many decided to also stop eating any other kind of meat, so now there are probably more vegetarians per capita in Israel than in any country other than India!

Carciofi alla Giuda

If carp is the Jewish contribution to French cuisine, this artichoke dish is its Italian counterpart. In fact, Italian Jews have been cooking with artichokes since before Roman times, and have many artichoke dishes. This one is the simplest and most basic, but it best brings out the flavor of the vegetable.

When buying artichokes, always look for leaves that are fat, glossy, and rounded. If the leaves become pointed, it means the artichokes are starting to shrivel and dry out.

pareve, kosher for Passover

SERVES 6

6 artichokes
2 lemons
2 tablespoons salt

1 teaspoon black pepper
3 cups olive oil

Trim the stems from the artichokes and discard them, or use them to make a vegetable broth. Prepare 2 large bowls of cold water. Cut the lemons in half and squeeze the juice into 1 bowl, then add the lemon halves to it. Put the artichokes into the other bowl.

Take an artichoke in your hand and trim around the edge of the bottom, discarding the outer leaves. Plunge the knife between the tightly closed central part and the tough outer leaves. Turn the artichoke in your hand and cut through the leaves in an upward spiral, so you are removing the tough tops of all the leaves while retaining the fleshy parts at the bottom. Drop each finished artichoke into the lemon water. Repeat for remaining artichokes.

Hit the base of an artichoke against your work surface to open up the leaves. Sprinkle with salt and pepper, including between the leaves. Repeat with the rest of the artichokes.

Heat the oil in a very large, deep pan large enough to hold all the artichokes. Pack the artichokes tightly in the pan in one layer. Reduce heat, cover the pan, and cook the artichokes for 5 minutes over medium heat. Have a bowl of water next to the pan.

After 5 minutes, sprinkle a little water over the artichokes in the pan and quickly recover the pan to prevent the steam from escaping. Repeat this procedure every 5 minutes until 25 minutes have elapsed. The artichokes should be cooked by now. To test, remove an artichoke from the pan. Turn it upside down and insert a knife into the base; if the knife slides in easily, the artichoke is cooked. Drain well to remove excess oil.

Eat the artichokes with the fingers, using a knife to remove the inedible choke when you get to it.

✡

Creamed Beets

This Polish dairy dish is a very suitable main course for Shavuot, the Feast of Weeks.

dairy, kosher for Passover

SERVES 8

2 pounds cooked beets
4 tablespoons butter
½ teaspoon salt

2 tablespoons wine vinegar
½ cup heavy cream

Peel and chop the beets. Heat half the butter in a skillet over high heat and sauté the beets for 5 minutes, stirring frequently. Sprinkle with salt and vinegar. In a small saucepan, melt the rest of the butter and pour it over the beets. Stir, then add the cream and stir again. Serve hot.

✡

Veal Rolls for the Sabbath; recipe on page 96

Brussels Sprouts with Chestnuts

This Dutch and Belgian dish is a delicious winter-vegetable accompaniment to a roast; it is especially good with turkey. The recipe is from my Great-Grandmother Milly (Amelia), whose family came to England from Holland.

Since chestnuts are often imported and can be very expensive in some parts of the United States, 2 cups of diced sweet potatoes make a very acceptable substitute, because the flavors are so similar.

meat, kosher for Passover

SERVES 8

2 cups (1 pound) chestnuts	1 tablespoon chicken fat
1½ pounds brussels sprouts	salt and black pepper

To cook the chestnuts, slit their skins with a paring knife and boil them in water to cover for 15 minutes. Remove a few at a time and when they are cool enough, peel off the skins with a sharp knife.

Put the peeled chestnuts in a saucepan with salted water to cover. Bring to a boil and continue to boil for 30 minutes or until tender. Drain chestnuts, reserving the water for soup.

Trim the brussels sprouts and cut a cross in the base of each to enable them to cook evenly. Bring a saucepan of salted water to a boil over high heat and add the brussels sprouts. Cook the brussels sprouts for 15 minutes or until tender.

Drain brussels sprouts and mix with chestnuts. Add the chicken fat and season with pepper. Serve hot.

Chicken with Olives; recipe on page 102

Carrot Tsimmes

Here is one of the many variations of this dish, which either accompanies a main course as a vegetable or, when cooked with the meat, is served as a stew. *Tsimmes* is also the Yiddish word for a "mess" or "muddle"! Carrots are traditional at Jewish New Year. This carrot mixture is often browned briefly under the broiler or in a hot oven before serving.

pareve, kosher for Passover

SERVES 4

2 pounds carrots	juice of ½ lemon
½ teaspoon salt	3 tablespoons margarine
⅔ cup honey	3 tablespoons matzo meal

Slice the carrots into ¼-inch rounds. Place them in a deep pot and add enough water to cover. Bring water to a boil over high heat and boil for 10 minutes, or until carrots are tender.

Add the salt, honey, and lemon juice, and simmer the mixture for 20 minutes, uncovered, or until the liquid is reduced by one-third. In a small saucepan, melt the margarine and stir in the matzo meal. When the mixture is smooth, stir it into the carrot mixture, and cook for 5 minutes more. Serve hot.

✡

Herbed Lentil Stew

Was this lentil stew the "mess of pottage" for which Esau sold his birthright? It is a typical Middle Eastern stew, this time from Lebanese Jews. It is a one-pot meal, a filling everyday entree.

pareve

SERVES 4

2 cups red lentils	1 pound spinach, trimmed and chopped
3 cups water	2 potatoes, peeled
2 tablespoons oil	juice of 1 lemon
1 large onion, sliced	½ teaspoon salt
2 garlic cloves, crushed	¼ teaspoon cayenne pepper
2 tablespoons chopped fresh coriander (cilantro)	

Wash the lentils and pick them over to remove any small stones or other impurities. Put lentils in a saucepan and add water. Bring to a boil over high heat, then reduce the heat, cover the pan, and cook for 20 minutes.

Heat the oil in a 2-quart heatproof casserole or Dutch oven. Add the onion and cook over medium heat until the onion is transparent, about 5 minutes. Add the garlic and coriander and cook 5 minutes more. Then add the spinach, and cook for another 5 minutes, stirring constantly.

Add the potatoes and lentils with their cooking liquid to the saucepan. Bring to a boil over a high heat, then reduce the heat, cover the pan, and simmer for 1 hour or until thick. Add the lemon juice, salt, and black pepper just before serving.

Stewed Okra

Okra is a popular vegetable among Middle Eastern and Sephardic Jews in Greece, Turkey, Romania, Africa, and parts of the Middle East, including Israel. Okra must always be trimmed carefully so that the seeds are not exposed or it will become very slimy during cooking.

pareve, kosher for Passover

SERVES 4

3 tablespoons olive oil	1 pound okra, trimmed
1 onion, halved, then thinly sliced length-wise	juice of ½ lemon
	1 teaspoon salt
4 large tomatoes, peeled and chopped, or 1 can (32 oz.) peeled tomatoes	¼ teaspoon black pepper

Heat the oil in a saucepan over high heat and sauté the onion until transparent, about 5 minutes. Add the tomatoes and okra and cook for 5 minutes. Add the remaining ingredients, cover the pan, reduce heat, and simmer for 30 minutes, checking that the liquid has not dried up. Add water if necessary. Serve hot or cold with pita bread.

Sweet-and-Sour Red Cabbage

This is a good accompaniment to strongly flavored meats, turkey, or even goose. Always cook the cabbage in a stainless-steel or enamel pot; aluminum will react with the acid in the vinegar and the sour salt.

pareve, kosher for Passover

SERVES 8

1 red cabbage, shredded	*½ cup golden raisins*
¾ cup water	*½ cup wine vinegar*
½ teaspoon salt	*2 tablespoons brown sugar*
2 large apples, peeled, cored, and diced	*dash of sour salt (citric acid)*

Put the cabbage, water, and salt in a large pot. Bring to a boil over high heat, then cover the pot and cook the cabbage for 15 minutes.

Add the remaining ingredients and cook until the cabbage is tender, about 20 minutes.

✡

Latkes

These delicious potato pancakes are traditional on Chanukah, the Festival of Lights. In many Sephardic communities and also in Italy, oil lamps are still used for the *menorah*, but in the Ashkenazic communities and in Israel, the oil has been replaced by candles. Oil is still an important part of the festival, however, as the cooking medium for the various Chanukah foods. Photo opposite page 124.

pareve

SERVES 8

2 pounds large potatoes	*1 egg, lightly beaten*
juice of ½ lemon	*salt and black pepper*
2 tablespoons all-purpose flour	*8 tablespoons oil*

Line a large bowl with cheesecloth, letting it fall over the outside edges. Grate the potatoes on a coarse grater into the bowl (or use the grating attachment on a food processor and transfer the potatoes to the bowl). Quickly sprinkle grated potatoes with lemon juice to prevent darkening. Cover the bowl and leave at room temperature for 30 minutes.

Gather up the ends of the cheesecloth and squeeze out the moisture. Hold the cheesecloth briefly under running water and squeeze again thoroughly to remove excess moisture.

Transfer the grated potatoes to a clean bowl. Stir in the flour, beaten egg, and salt and pepper. Heat the oil in a skillet over high heat. Drop 2 tablespoons of the mixture into the hot oil and cook until browned, turning halfway through the cooking, about 4 minutes on each side. Fry latkes in batches. Drain them on absorbent paper, then keep warm. Serve hot with pastrami, or as a dessert for a dairy entree, with sour cream and applesauce.

Roast Potatoes with Rice

This traditional Sephardic dish has always accompanied roast beef or lamb in our house. Baked in an ovenproof glass dish, it can be brought directly from the stove to the table, and is a favorite of my mother, Kate Evelyn Hackman.

meat

SERVES 8

5 large potatoes, peeled	salt and black pepper
2 cups uncooked rice	½ cup chicken fat or shortening
1 onion, grated	about 3 cups hot chicken broth

Preheat oven to 400°F. Halve the potatoes lengthwise and then crosswise to divide them into quarters. Cover the bottom of a 2-inch-deep, 2-quart rectangular ovenproof baking dish with the rice.

Sprinkle rice with onion, then arrange the potatoes in rows standing on their flat bases like miniature pyramids. Dot the tops of the potatoes with the chicken fat.

Pour enough chicken broth into the baking dish to come to just below the top. Put dish in oven and bake for 1 hour, checking liquid every 15 minutes. If liquid has evaporated, add a little more until the rice is cooked (taste to test), then stop adding liquid and continue cooking until both tops of the potatoes and rice are golden brown.

Aloo Makala

The Beni Israel Jews of India lived mainly in Bombay, although many emigrated to Israel. These potatoes are traditional for Friday night dinner, served with Indian Stewed Chicken (page 101). Grape-seed oil is not traditional in India, but it is a light oil suitable for this kind of deep-frying, and is one of the most healthful of all the cooking oils. It is available in stores on the West Coast and natural foods stores in the rest of the country. If not available, substitute safflower oil.

This recipe is from Sarah Avraham, a Beni Israel Jew.

pareve, kosher for Passover

SERVES 8

3 pounds new potatoes, of uniform size	*1 teaspoon salt*
½ teaspoon turmeric	*2 cups safflower or grape-seed oil*

Scrape the potatoes to remove the skins. Bring a large saucepan of water to a boil over high heat. Add the turmeric and salt, and then the potatoes. Bring the water back to a boil and cook potatoes for 5 minutes.

Drain and let potatoes dry on absorbent paper. Heat the oil in a deep 2-quart pan or flameproof casserole. Place potatoes in the oil and cook over high heat for 3 minutes. Reduce heat and continue cooking, lightly turning the potatoes to prevent sticking, until they start to wrinkle. Increase the heat again and cook, turning them so they cook evenly, until they are golden brown and soft, about 10 minutes. Drain the potatoes on absorbent paper and keep warm until ready to serve.

Potato Kugel

This comes from Byelorussia, a province in western Russia that had a large prewar Jewish population. Potato kugel is a rich, hearty savory pudding—almost a meal in itself.

pareve, kosher for Passover

SERVES 8

6 large potatoes, peeled and quartered
¼ cup margarine
3 onions, chopped
2 eggs, lightly beaten
3 tablespoons fine matzo meal

1 teaspoon baking powder
½ teaspoon salt
½ teaspoon black pepper
pinch of grated nutmeg

Boil the potatoes in water to cover until they are cooked, about 20 minutes. Drain and mash them.

Preheat oven to 400°F. Grease a 2-quart casserole dish. Melt the margarine in a skillet and sauté the onions until they are transparent, about 5 minutes. Pour the onions and fat over the potatoes and mix well. Mix in the spices. Put the mixture into the baking dish. Bake for 45 minutes or until crust is golden brown.

✡

Minas

This Passover leek and potato pie is very popular among Greek and Turkish Jews. It contains leeks, so popular in Biblical times, which means that it is probably a very old recipe. The cheese in the recipe is *katchkeval*, a goat cheese from Turkey and Greece that is available in specialty stores. If hard to find, use any strong yellow cheese, such as colby, monterey jack, or sharp cheddar. The leeks need a very thorough washing, as sand collects in their numerous layers.

dairy, kosher for Passover

SERVES 6 TO 8

2 pounds leeks, white parts only, cut in
    short pieces
4 large potatoes, peeled
1 teaspoon salt
4 tablespoons butter
2 tablespoons plain yogurt
1 onion, chopped

1 cup grated katchkeval cheese
6 matzos
1 tablespoon oil
4 eggs, lightly beaten
½ teaspoon black pepper
2 tablespoons milk

Place the leeks, potatoes, and half the salt in water to cover and boil until tender, about 20 minutes. Drain, reserving the water for soup or broth.

Mash the potatoes with half the butter and the yogurt. Melt the remaining butter in a skillet over high heat and sauté the onion until golden, about 5 minutes. Stir onion into the mashed potatoes along with the leeks and half the cheese.

Preheat the oven to 400°F. Thoroughly butter a deep 2 quart baking dish. Put 3 of the matzos in the dish and sprinkle with water to soften them. Leave for a few minutes, then press them up the sides of the dish. Pile the potato mixture into the center and sprinkle with the remaining cheese and yogurt. Cover with the remaining matzos and sprinkle them again lightly with water to soften. Sprinkle the matzos with the oil, then bake the dish, uncovered, for 20 minutes.

Beat the eggs with the black pepper and milk, then pour mixture over the potato mixture. Bake 10 additional minutes, then sprinkle with the remaining cheese. Bake for a further 10 minutes, then serve hot or cold.

Vegetarian Cholent

If desired, add a few raw eggs in their shells to this stew at the simmering stage for extra nourishment.

pareve, can be slow-cooked for Sabbath

SERVES 8

2½ cups lima, navy, or great northern
    beans
2 white turnips, quartered
2 yellow turnips, quartered
1 large onion, quartered
6 potatoes, peeled
2 cups canned or fresh tomatoes, peeled
1 bunch fresh parsley
1 bunch fresh coriander (cilantro)

¾ cup wine vinegar
1 teaspoon paprika
½ teaspoon dried thyme
1 bay leaf
½ teaspoon ground cumin
½ teaspoon black pepper
1 clove garlic, chopped
1 teaspoon salt

Soak the beans in water to cover overnight. Drain well and add to a saucepan. Cover with fresh water. Bring to a boil over medium heat. Cook for 10 minutes, then add remaining ingredients except salt. Cover pot, reduce heat, and simmer mixture for at least 2 hours or until beans are tender. Alternately, you could bake mixture for at least 4 hours in an oven set on 250°F. Add salt 10 minutes before serving, and serve hot.

Israeli Salad

pareve, kosher for Passover

SERVES 4

2 large tomatoes
1 long or 2 short cucumbers
1 green bell pepper
4 tablespoons chopped fresh parsley

2 tablespoons salad or olive oil
1 lemon
salt and black pepper

Chop the tomatoes into tiny cubes about ¼ inch square. Peel the cucumber and chop in the same way. Core the bell pepper and cut it lengthwise. Scrape out and discard the seeds, then chop the pepper into tiny pieces, the same size as the tomatoes and cucumber.

Toss the cubed vegetables together with the parsley, then sprinkle with the oil and toss again. Cut the lemon in half and squeeze the juice from both halves into the salad. Toss again and serve immediately.

9

DESSERTS

Milkless desserts take some ingenuity, so I have included as many as possible. Nowadays there are various vegetable products, such as tofu and creamed coconut, which can be used as milk or cream would be in a recipe. However, many Orthodox Jews feel uncomfortable when served what *appears* to be a dairy dessert at a meat meal. A kosher New York restaurant started serving a "cheesecake" made with tofu and entirely without milk, but they had some very angry customers. Still, it's not so long ago that using milkless margarine, which tasted just like butter, was felt to be cheating.

By far the most popular dessert after a heavy festival or Sabbath meal is a dried fruit compote, so I shall begin with that.

Dried Fruit Compote

Any combination of dried fruits can be used, and the spicing varied to taste. Don't cook compote in an aluminum pan; the acid in the fruits will react with the pan.

pareve, kosher for Passover

SERVES 12

1 cup pitted prunes	½ cup sugar
1 cup dried apricots	juice of 1 lemon
½ cup dried peaches	about 2 quarts water
1 cup dried pears	4 whole cloves
½ cup dried apple rings	1 stick cinnamon
½ cup raisins	12 blanched almonds for garnish

Put the dried fruits into a large pan with the sugar and lemon juice. Add the water (enough to generously cover the fruit). Bring to a boil over high heat.

Meanwhile, tie the cloves and cinnamon stick in a piece of cheesecloth and put them in the pan with the fruit. Cover the pan, and reduce heat to very low. Simmer the fruit for 20 minutes.

Remove pan from the heat, discard the cheesecloth bag, and pour the fruit into a glass serving bowl. Add almonds for decoration. Chill before serving.

VARIATION

When the fruit is cooked, strain the liquid and set fruit aside. Mix liquid with 2 envelopes kosher gelatin and stir to dissolve. Let cool, then add the fruit before gelatin sets. Serve with cream for dairy meals or Almond Custard (page 124) for meat meals.

Melon Fruit Salad

Israel's Ogen melons are small, similar to a cantaloupe. They are named for the kibbutz on which they were first grown. This dessert, which can also be served as a first course, is popular because these tiny, 2-portion melons are so readily available.

pareve, kosher for Passover

SERVES 4

2 very small cantaloupes
8 ounces green grapes
8 ounces red grapes
4 ripe peaches

1 teaspoon ground cinnamon
1 cup unsweetened grape juice or dry red
  wine

Cut the melons in half; scrape out and discard the seeds. Scoop out and reserve the melon flesh, being careful not to pierce the skin. If possible, use a melon baller to cut the flesh into small balls; otherwise, cut it into small, neat cubes.

Save 4 tiny clusters of red grapes for a garnish. Remove the rest from their stems and cut in half. Discard any seeds. Plunge the peaches in a bowl of boiling water for 2 minutes, remove with a slotted spoon, and let cool. When cool enough to handle, peel them, slipping skin off. Cut them into small pieces.

Combine the melon pieces, grapes, peaches, and cinnamon in a bowl. Stir in the grape juice or wine. Spoon the mixture back into the melon shells and top with reserved grape clusters.

Pomegranates and Almonds

This delicious dessert is traditional in North Africa at the Jewish New Year. Rosebuds are available from Middle Eastern stores, as are rosewater or orange-flower water.

pareve, kosher for Passover

SERVES 4

2 pomegranates
1 cup chopped blanched almonds
¼ cup sugar

4 drops orange-flower water or rosewater
dried rosebuds or rose petals to decorate
(optional)

Break open the pomegranates and carefully remove the sacs enclosing the juice and seeds. Discard all the white parts of the fruit; they are very bitter. Place pomegranate in a bowl. Carefully stir in the almonds, sugar, and orange-flower or rosewater, taking care not to break the sacs. Divide the mixture among 4 dessert bowls or sundae glasses. Sprinkle with the rosebuds or rose petals, and serve chilled.

Strawberry Auflauf

A delicious soufflé originally from Austro-Hungary, this recipe can also be prepared with other soft berries such as raspberries, loganberries, boysenberries, or blueberries.

pareve

SERVES 8

1 pound very ripe strawberries
6 eggs, separated
1¼ cups sugar, plus extra for coating
    dish

4 tablespoons graham cracker crumbs

Preheat the oven to 325°F. Rinse a 2-quart soufflé dish with water, then sprinkle with sugar.

Puree the strawberries in a blender or food processor. Beat the egg yolks with the sugar until the mixture is pale yellow. Combine the egg-yolk mixture with the pureed strawberries.

Beat the egg whites until they form stiff peaks, then fold them into the strawberry mixture along with the graham cracker crumbs. Pour the mixture into the prepared dish and place in a larger pan filled with hot water.

Bake for 30 minutes, or until soufflé is well risen. It will have a thin cooked crust but be fairly liquid in the center while hot, stiffening up as it cools.

Let soufflé cool, then unmold. Serve hot or cold.

VARIATION

For Passover, substitute coarse matzo meal or cooked matzo farfel for the graham cracker crumbs.

✡

Cheese Blintzes

These cheese pancakes are standard fare for Shavuot. *Blintz* is a Yiddish word, and these pancakes are traditional among all Ashkenazic Jews. Photo opposite page 125.

dough: pareve; filling: dairy

SERVES 6

about ¾ cup butter for frying

BLINTZ DOUGH
2 eggs
½ cup all-purpose flour
½ teaspoon salt
½ cup milk

FILLING
¾ pound cottage cheese
1 egg yolk, lightly beaten
grated rind of 1 lemon
2 tablespoons sugar
4 tablespoons raisins

In a bowl, combine ingredients for the batter and chill for at least 30 minutes. Combine filling ingredients in another bowl.

Lightly grease a skillet, omelet, or crepe pan and place over high heat. Add a large tablespoon of batter and tip the pan so the batter spreads from side to side to cover the bottom. Cook on 1 side for about 2 minutes, or until the batter loosens around the sides of the crepe. Remove from pan and place on absorbent paper. Repeat until all the batter is used up, lightly greasing pan between each crepe.

Place a rounded tablespoon of the filling down the center of each pancake. Fold the long sides toward the center to keep the filling from escaping, and roll up each pancake. Melt remaining butter in the skillet and brown the blintzes over medium heat. Serve with applesauce or with sour cream, sugar, and cinnamon.

Cherry Kreplach

These are traditional at Shavuot, which happily occurs when cherries are in season. Instead of using canned cherries, stew a pound of fresh cherries in 1 cup water and sugar to taste. Don't overcook them.

Kreplach are given different shapes in different places. Polish Jews often fold them into ear-shaped pieces (*uzhki*), while others shape them like ravioli. When the dough pockets are made in half-moons, they are called cherry *varnishkes*. To make pareve cherry kreplach, boil the cherry syrup with 2 teaspoons cornstarch until thickened, then let cool before using.

dough: pareve; filling: dairy

SERVES 8

DOUGH
2 eggs
½ cup water
about 5 cups all-purpose flour
½ teaspoon salt
1 teaspoon sugar

FILLING AND TOPPING
1 can (16 ounces) pitted sweet cherries
1 cup sour cream
½ cup confectioners sugar

In a large bowl, beat the eggs with the water until smooth. Gradually add 3 cups of the flour and the salt and sugar, beating constantly to form a stiff dough.

Sprinkle your work surface generously with flour. Turn out the dough, and knead thoroughly, adding more flour if necessary, until it no longer sticks to your hands or the work surface. Cover dough with a damp cloth and let rest at room temperature for at least 30 minutes.

Roll out dough on a floured surface and use a wine glass or cookie cutter to cut out 3-inch rounds of dough. Drain the cherries and place 2 cherries on each round. Fold the dough in half like a turnover. Moisten the edges and pinch them together, or press with the tines of a fork to seal.

Bring a large pot of water to a boil over high heat. Add the kreplach and bring back to a boil. Reduce heat to prevent the water from boiling over, then increase heat again and cook for 5 minutes. Drain the kreplach, then serve with sour cream and cinnamon. If pareve, serve sprinkled with confectioners sugar.

Almond Custard

There are many ways of substituting for cream. You could use sweetened coconut milk, or beat tofu with a little sugar in a blender until smooth, or use soybean milk. This is an old-fashioned but more delicious way. Although a Russian recipe, it bears a striking resemblance to Chinese almond pudding! Don't use commercial ready-ground or blanched almonds; they will be too dry to produce good milk. To blanch the almonds, soak in boiling water for a few minutes, then squeeze the skins off and dry well.

pareve, kosher for Passover

SERVES 4

1 pound blanched almonds	4 drops almond extract
½ cup sugar	1 envelope kosher gelatin
½ cup potato starch	4 tablespoons water

Grind the almonds in a food processor, then put in a saucepan and add water to cover. Bring to a boil over high heat and boil, uncovered, for 10 minutes. Allow to cool slightly. Rinse a large piece of cheesecloth in cold water. Arrange several layers of the cheesecloth over a bowl and strain the almond milk through it.

Combine the almond milk with the sugar and potato starch in a saucepan. Simmer over low heat, stirring frequently, until thickened, then remove from heat.

Dissolve the gelatin in the water and add to the almond milk. Pour mixture into a bowl and let cool, then chill. Serve alone as a dessert or use instead of cream to accompany other puddings.

Latkes; recipe on page 11

Fruited Rice Auflauf

This is a popular dessert among German and Austrian Jews. It can be made dairy by cooking the rice in milk and using butter instead of margarine. However if you switch it to dairy, use canned, not fresh, pineapple. Fresh pineapple will curdle the milk and spoil the pudding.

pareve

SERVES 6 TO 8

2 cups long-grain rice	2 peeled peaches, fresh or canned,
6 cups water	chopped
1 cup sugar	2 pineapple rings, chopped
½ teaspoon grated nutmeg	1 tablespoon golden raisins
1 teaspoon ground cloves	2 eggs, separated
1 teaspoon vanilla extract	2 tablespoons margarine

Place the rice in a saucepan. Add the water and bring to a boil. Cover and reduce heat; cook until soft, about 20 minutes.

Stir half the sugar, all the spices, vanilla, chopped fruits, raisins, and egg yolks into the rice. Whip the egg whites with the remaining sugar until stiff, then fold into the rice.

Preheat the oven to 350°F. Lightly grease a 2-quart glass baking dish. Turn the rice mixture into prepared dish. Cut the margarine into pieces and use to dot the top of the pudding. Bake for 40 minutes, or until lightly browned on top. Serve hot or chilled.

Persian Rose Pudding

This is another delicious rice pudding, eaten by the Jews of Teheran on Shavuot, which they also call the Festival of Roses. Dried rosebuds and rosewater, which are used throughout the Middle East and North Africa, are sold in Middle Eastern groceries. Rosewater syrup is available and is delicious with this pudding.

dairy

SERVES 6 TO 8

6 cups water
2 cups long-grain or medium-grain rice
2 eggs
2 cups milk
1¼ cups chopped pitted dates

2 tablespoons sugar
2 teaspoons rosewater
dash of ground cinnamon
4 tablespoons butter
dried or fresh rosebuds for garnish

Place the water in a saucepan and add the rice. Bring to a boil over high heat, and when the rice starts to "dance," reduce heat and cover pan. Cook 15 minutes, or until rice is tender. Drain off any remaining water and let cool for a few minutes.

Preheat the oven to 350°F. Butter a deep 2-quart glass baking dish.

Beat the eggs until foamy. Add the milk, dates, sugar, rosewater, and cinnamon. Pour over the rice and blend well. Transfer mixture to the prepared dish, then cut the butter into small pieces and dot over the rice. Bake pudding for 40 minutes, or until lightly browned.

Remove pudding from the oven and let cool. Unmold onto a serving platter and decorate with the rosebuds. Chill until ready to serve, and serve with rosewater syrup or cream.

Noodles with Nuts

Believe it or not, this is a breakfast dish! I saw it on the breakfast menu of a Hungarian restaurant in Jerusalem and was shocked. For those with conservative breakfast tastes, however, it makes a great, quick dessert.

pareve

SERVES 4

8 ounces egg noodles
2 cups water
¼ teaspoon salt
½ cup ground walnuts

1 teaspoon ground cinnamon
½ cup packed brown sugar
½ cup margarine, melted

Boil the noodles in the salted water for 10 minutes. Drain noodles well. Combine the walnuts and cinnamon in a bowl with the sugar. Serve a portion of noodles to each guest and let them help themselves to the nut mixture.

✡

Babanatza

A Passover pudding popular in Romania and Bulgaria, this is served as either a dessert or an accompaniment to meat.

pareve, kosher for Passover

SERVES 6 TO 8

6 matzos
1 cup raisins
6 eggs
1 cup coarsely chopped walnuts
2 green apples, peeled, cored, and diced

¼ cup oil
½ cup honey
¼ cup sugar
2 tablespoons margarine, cut in pieces
1 teaspoon ground cinnamon

Break the matzos into pieces. Pour a little boiling water over to soften them, then squeeze out the excess moisture. Mix matzos with the raisins and eggs in a bowl.

Mix the walnuts and apples in another bowl with the oil, honey, and sugar. Add this mixture to the matzo mixture and stir well.

Preheat the oven to 350°F. Grease a deep 1½-quart ovenproof dish and pour the mixture in. Sprinkle with cinnamon, then bake pudding for 1 hour. Serve warm, or chill and serve with applesauce.

VARIATION

Instead of baking the mixture, deep-fry it in tablespoonfuls in hot (350°F) oil. These are called *gremsel* or *frimsel* and are from Central and Eastern Europe.

Sweet Fruit Kugel

This Ashkenazic recipe from Austro-Hungary and Poland is baked overnight with the Sabbath stew. The better quality the leftover bread or cake, the more delicious the kugel. Serve it with Dried Fruit Compote (page 119) or Almond Custard (page 124).

pareve
can be slow-cooked for Sabbath

SERVES 8

8 cups crumbled stale bread or cake
   (about 10 slices)
4 tablespoons water
6 tablespoons sweet red wine
2 eggs, lightly beaten
2 apples, peeled, cored, and chopped
2 pears, peeled, cored, and chopped
6 plums or prunes, pitted and chopped

4 tablespoons raisins
1 lemon, rind grated and juice squeezed
1 teaspoon ground cinnamon
1 teaspoon ground allspice
½ teaspoon ground cloves
½ teaspoon salt
½ cup chicken fat or shortening

Preheat oven to 250°F. Grease a 2-quart baking dish.

Sprinkle the bread or cake with the water and half the wine; mash lightly with a fork. Combine the beaten eggs with the chopped fruit, lemon rind and juice, spices, and salt. Pour fruit mixture over the softened bread or cake. Melt 2 tablespoons of the fat and stir it into the mixture, then turn mixture into prepared baking dish and bake overnight in a very low oven—about 250°F—or place dish in a roasting pan half-filled with hot water and bake at least 4 hours.

Matzos Shalet

The shalet, or schaleth, is a traditional sweet pudding eaten by Ashkenazic Jews. The word is actually a corruption of *cholent*, and refers to when the pudding was cooked like the kugel with the Sabbath stew. When the famous 19th-century French chef Antonin Carême invented the charlotte pudding, confusion deepened. Some Jewish cookbooks call this dessert a charlotte, though it has little in common with that creation of *haute cuisine*.

pareve, kosher for Passover

SERVES 6

2 large matzos
3 eggs, separated
1/2 cup margarine, cut in small pieces
1/2 cup brown sugar
2 cups sliced apples

4 tablespoons finely chopped or ground
  almonds
4 tablespoons raisins
1/2 teaspoon ground cinnamon
pinch of salt

Soak the matzos in a little cold water until they are softened, then squeeze out excess moisture.

Preheat the oven to 350°F. Grease a 1-quart baking dish or casserole.

Beat the egg yolks in a large bowl until foamy. Add the matzos, margarine, brown sugar, apples, almonds, raisins, and cinnamon. Beat the egg whites with a pinch of salt until they form stiff peaks, then fold into the fruit mixture. Pour mixture into the prepared dish and bake for 45 minutes, or until golden brown.

Lokshen Kugel

Most people find this Ashkenazic pudding a little heavy after a big meal, but it could always be eaten at teatime on its own or as a midnight snack. It is just as good cold as hot.

pareve

SERVES 6

8 ounces broad egg noodles
3 eggs, separated
1 teaspoon ground cinnamon
1/4 teaspoon grated nutmeg
3/4 cup raisins

1/2 cup sugar
3 tablespoons shortening
pinch of salt
about 4 tablespoons brown sugar

Preheat the oven to 350°F. Grease a 2-quart ovenproof basin or baking dish.

Fill a large pan with salted boiling water and cook noodles until soft, about 12 minutes. Drain noodles and rinse under cold water.

In a large bowl, combine the egg yolks with the cinnamon, nutmeg, raisins, and sugar. Add the noodles and shortening, and mix well. Whip the egg whites with the salt until they form stiff peaks. Fold the whites into the noodle mixture, then pour into prepared dish. Put dish in oven and bake for 45 minutes, or until golden brown. Sprinkle with brown sugar and serve hot.

✡

Persian Purim Halva

The halva in the Middle East is a mixture of ground sesame seeds, almonds, or even peanuts and honey; it is best made commercially in huge blocks. This dessert from the Iranian Jews of Meshhed bears a strong similarity to an Indian sweet known as *hulwa*. The words *halva* and *hulwa* simply mean "sweet." The pudding is sent to friends and neighbors as one of the small food gifts customarily exchanged at Purim. The recipe is courtesy of Hannah Levy, formerly of Meshhed.

pareve

SERVES 8

2 tablespoons oil	*1 teaspoon ground cardamom*
2 cups medium-grain rice	*⅛ teaspoon saffron strands*
4 cups water	*½ cup boiling water*
½ cup sugar	*pomegranate seeds for garnish*
1 teaspoon ground cinnamon	

Heat the oil in a large skillet over high heat and fry the rice until it is lightly browned. Transfer to a heavy-based saucepan, add water and all but 1 tablespoon of the sugar, and the spices except saffron. Cook over very low heat, stirring frequently, until mixture is smooth, about 45 minutes.

In a bowl, mash the reserved sugar with the saffron and add boiling water. Stir this mixture into the rice and continue to cook, stirring, for 10 minutes. Let cool, then pour into individual bowls and chill. Garnish with pomegranate seeds and serve.

Juditha

Ice creams and iced puddings are as popular among Jews as anyone. Owing to dietary constraints, water ices are eaten more often than true ice cream. There is no "traditional" ice cream recipe, however this version has a most interesting history.

The following is a typical Victorian iced pudding. A recipe for Juditha appears in *The Jewish Manual*, written by "a lady." The name of the recipe is the clue to the identity of the lady, for it can be none other than Lady Judith Montefiore, wife of Sir Moses, a leader of the Orthodox community. If you cannot get fresh gooseberries, use canned and omit the sugar, or substitute a tart berry such as loganberries, which will need half the cooking time of gooseberries.

Make the ice cream and filling in layers if you do not have a big enough freezer to hold the bowl or mold. Use the leftover egg whites to make meringues or other cookies and serve them with the dessert.

dairy

SERVES 12

red or green glacéed cherries for garnish

BROWN BREAD ICE CREAM
5 cups heavy cream
1 vanilla bean
3 egg yolks, lightly beaten
1 cup soft brown sugar
2 cups fresh brown breadcrumbs

GOOSEBERRY SORBET
1 pound fresh gooseberries, trimmed
1 cup water
½ cup sugar
3 egg yolks

To make the ice cream, place the cream and vanilla bean in a saucepan over low heat, bring to a boil, stirring occasionally, then let cool slightly. Beat the egg yolks and sugar together until foamy, then pour cream over, beating constantly with a wire whisk until well blended. Transfer mixture to a double-boiler and cook until it thickens, stirring frequently, about 10 minutes; do not let mixture boil. Let cool, then pour into a 2-quart metal bowl and place in freezer. When half frozen, remove from freezer and beat mixture to break up the crystals. Freeze again until solid.

While the ice cream is freezing, place the gooseberries in a saucepan and add water. Cook over low heat until soft, about 15 minutes. Remove from heat and let cool slightly. Beat the sugar and egg yolks until foamy, then pour gooseberries onto the mixture and blend well. Puree the mixture in a food processor or blender, then chill the gooseberry sorbet until very cold.

Scoop out a large hollow in the center of the ice cream, leaving a shell about 1 inch thick. Pour the sorbet into the hollow and return to freezer for 2 hours, or until the sorbet has begun to set. Freeze the ice cream that was removed separately.

After 2 hours, cover sorbet in center with the ice cream that was scooped out. If any is left over, there are sure to be plenty of volunteers to take care of it, or serve it at another meal. To unmold, stand the bowl, flat side down, on a serving plate. Rinse a kitchen towel in hot water and wrap it round the mold, then lift up. The mold should come off easily; if not, rinse the towel again and repeat. Decorate the Juditha with candied cherries, then serve.

VARIATION

To make this a pareve dish to follow a meat meal, substitute unsweetened coconut milk or soybean milk for the heavy cream, or use sweetened coconut milk and omit the sugar.

10

CAKES, PASTRIES, AND COOKIES

I have put cakes, pastries, and cookies in a separate chapter, since in many countries cakes are not actually desserts. In the Austro-Hungarian Empire, cakes and luscious pastries were consumed with morning coffee or at teatime; in the Middle East and North Africa, they are snacks, eaten during the day with strong, finely ground Turkish coffee; in Britain and the British Empire, they are eaten at teatime. These customs have been adopted by Jews.

Probably the only cakes that can be said to be truly Jewish in origin are those made with flour substitutes for Passover. Yet we associate many other cakes with Jewish cooking because it was the Jews from Eastern and Central Europe who set up bakeries and popularized these delicious baked goods.

Classic Cheesecake

Here is a good example of a cake everyone associates with Jews although it is not intrinsically Jewish. Cheese and other dairy dishes are always eaten on Shavuot, however this type of cake owes more to the Germans and Austrians and less to the Jews, who have adopted it and made it their own. It has the spongy consistency of the traditional cheesecake, not the heavier, puddinglike texture of newer American-style cheesecakes.

dairy

SERVES 8

6 tablespoons unsalted butter	2 cups sour cream
2 cups graham cracker crumbs	1 cup sugar
½ teaspoon ground cinnamon	juice and grated rind of 1 lemon
6 eggs, separated	1 teaspoon vanilla extract
1 pound cream cheese	2 tablespoons all-purpose flour

Preheat the oven to 350°F. Grease the bottom and sides of a 9-inch springform pan.

Melt the butter, then combine with the graham cracker crumbs and cinnamon in a bowl. Press the crumbs into the bottom and about ½ inch up the sides of the pan. Save a few crumbs for the topping.

Combine the egg yolks, cream cheese, sour cream, sugar, lemon juice and rind, vanilla, and flour in a large bowl. Beat well until light and fluffy. Beat the egg whites until they form stiff peaks, then fold them into the cream cheese mixture. Pour batter into the prepared pan and sprinkle top with the remaining crumbs.

Bake the cake for 1 hour, then turn off the oven and leave cake in for another hour. Then open oven door and leave ajar for 30 minutes before removing cake. Refrigerate and serve chilled.

Passover Matzo-Layer Cake

This simple recipe, which seems to be an Israeli invention, is easy enough for a child to make and incredibly delicious.

dairy, kosher for Passover

SERVES 10

6 tablespoons sugar
4 ounces unsweetened chocolate
1 cup + 2 tablespoons water
½ cup butter or margarine, cut in pieces
6 ounces halva, cut in small pieces

½ cup sweet red wine
2 tablespoons potato starch
6 large matzos
sprinkles for decoration

Put the sugar and chocolate in a saucepan and add 1 cup water. Bring to a boil over low heat, stirring constantly with a wooden spoon. Add the butter or margarine, halva, and wine. Continue stirring until the mixture boils again, then remove the pan from the heat.

Mix the potato starch with remaining 2 tablespoons water, then stir starch into the chocolate mixture. Return pan to the heat and cook over low heat, stirring until the mixture thickens, about 8 minutes. Remove from the heat.

Put one of the matzos on a platter large enough for it to lie flat. Use a metal spatula to spread a thin, even layer of the chocolate mixture over the matzo. Place another matzo on top and spread it with more chocolate. Repeat with the remaining matzos, finishing with a chocolate layer. Scatter sprinkles over the cake. Chill before serving, and do not eat until the following day. To serve, cut the cake into small rectangles about 1 inch by 2 inches, using a long, sharp knife.

Plava Cake

This is a traditional Passover spongecake—light, fluffy, and equally good at any time of the year.

pareve, kosher for Passover

SERVES 6 TO 8

6 eggs, separated	grated zest of 1 orange
1 cup sugar	pinch of ground cinnamon
1 cup fine matzo meal	¼ cup orange juice
½ cup ground blanched almonds	almond halves for decoration

Preheat the oven to 350°F. Grease an 8-inch round cake pan.

Beat the yolks with half the sugar in a large bowl until light yellow. Beat the egg whites until they form stiff peaks. Fold in remaining sugar. Fold egg whites into the beaten yolks.

Sift together the matzo meal, ground almonds, grated orange zest, and cinnamon, then add to the eggs, a tablespoon at a time, alternating with the orange juice. Fold gently to keep the mixture fluffy. Pour batter into prepared pan and top with the almond halves. Bake for 1 hour, or until golden brown. Let cool for 10 minutes, then remove from pan and let cool completely on a wire rack.

Chocolate Yeast Roll

This cake, called *ugat shemarim*, is baked in many Israeli Ashkenazic homes for the Sabbath. It is very easy to make.

pareve

SERVES 10 TO 12

1 envelope active dry yeast, or ½ cake compressed yeast	2 eggs, at room temperature, lightly beaten
⅔ cup sugar	½ cup unsweetened cocoa
1 cup lukewarm water	1 teaspoon ground cinnamon
4 cups all-purpose flour	2 tablespoons sugar dissolved in 1 teaspoon warm water
¼ teaspoon salt	
4 tablespoons margarine, melted	

Blend the yeast with 1 teaspoon sugar, then add lukewarm water. Cover with plastic wrap and leave in a warm place to rise for 20 minutes.

Sift the flour and salt into a warmed bowl. Make a well in the center, and pour in the yeast mixture. Stir in the melted margarine and eggs into the yeast mixture and gradually add the flour, beating until the dough is smooth. Knead the dough on a floured board until it no longer sticks to your fingers, about 10 minutes. Transfer dough to a greased bowl and cover with plastic wrap. Let rise in a warm place until doubled in bulk, 1 hour.

Roll dough out into a rectangle about ½ inch thick. Combine the cocoa, remaining sugar, and cinnamon, then sprinkle the mixture over the surface of the dough leaving a ½-inch border so the filling does not escape. Roll up the dough as for a jelly roll, transfer roll to a cookie sheet, and let rise in a warm place for 45 minutes. Preheat oven to 375°F. Brush dough with the sugar and water mixture, and bake for 1 hour or until golden brown.

✡

Bola

Bola is the Spanish word for a ball. It is also the name of a particular cake, presumably because the cake is made from a ball of dough. The standard bola is made from a yeast dough. Italian Jews have a version they call *bollo*, brought to them by Spanish Jews in the 15th century, which they eat on Sukkot and to break the fast on the Day of Atonement. *The Jewish Manual*, a 19th-century English cookbook, has recipes for 4 kinds of bola: a plain bola, *bola toliedo*, *bola de hispaniola*, and *bola d'amor*. (The latter is nothing like the standard bola but, rather, an incredibly elaborate confection layers of egg yolks and sugar, decorated with myrtle and gold leaf!)

pareve

SERVES 10 TO 12 (2 CAKES)

1 envelope active dry yeast, or ½ cake
   compressed yeast
⅔ cup sugar
1 cup lukewarm water
4 cups all-purpose flour
¼ teaspoon salt
1 cup margarine, softened
2 eggs

1 cup chopped candied peel
½ cup chopped candied ginger
2 tablespoons soft brown sugar
2 teaspoons ground cinnamon
1 cup ground almonds
3 tablespoons water
orange-flower water (optional)
sugar sprinkles for decoration

Mix the yeast with 1 teaspoon sugar, then add lukewarm water. Cover with plastic wrap and let rise in a warm place for 20 minutes.

Sift the flour and salt into a warmed bowl. Make a well in the center and pour in the yeast mixture. Lightly cover the bowl with a kitchen towel and leave for 15 minutes.

Warm 4 tablespoons of the margarine, then stir the margarine and eggs into the yeast mixture and gradually add the flour, beating until the dough is smooth. Knead dough on a floured board until it no longer sticks to your fingers, about 10 minutes. Transfer dough to a greased bowl and cover with plastic wrap. Let rise in a warm place until doubled in bulk, about 1 hour.

Chop the peel and ginger. (If the ginger is in syrup, reserve syrup.) Mix the peel and ginger with the brown sugar, cinnamon, and ground almonds.

Roll out dough into a round about ½ inch thick. Spread with half the remaining butter. Fold dough in half and roll out again into a round about ½ inch thick. Spread with remaining butter and fold. Cut dough in 4 pieces, and roll each out into an 8-inch round. Warm two 8-inch round cake pans, then line each with a round of dough. Cover each round with the peel-and-almond mixture and cover with the remaining rounds of dough. Cover with a cloth and let rise in a warm place for 45 minutes.

Preheat oven to 425°F and bake cakes for 30 minutes. Meanwhile, place in a saucepan the remaining sugar, the water, and 1 tablespoon of liquid from the preserved ginger; if using dry ginger, add a few drops orange-flower water. Put over medium heat, and boil the syrup for 10 minutes. Brush dough with the syrup, then continue to bake for another 30 minutes. Remove cakes from the oven, brush again with syrup, and decorate with sprinkles.

Iced Poppyseed Roll

This is a good cake to have on hand to serve unexpected visitors. Prune or nut filling can be substituted for poppyseed, if desired; for instructions on making the filling from scratch, see the recipe for Hamantaschen (page 148). Photo opposite page 140.

dairy

SERVES 8 TO 10

1 envelope active dry yeast
½ cup tepid milk
1 tablespoon granulated sugar
2 cups all-purpose flour
½ cup butter or margarine, softened

1 can (12½ ounces) poppyseed filling
2 cups confectioners sugar
1 egg white, lightly beaten
1 teaspoon lemon juice

To make the dough, place the yeast in a small bowl and add the warm milk, sugar, and 1 tablespoon of the flour. Stir to dissolve, then set mixture in a warm place, lightly covered with a cloth, until it foams, about 20 minutes.

Grease a cookie sheet. In a large bowl, cream the remaining sugar with the butter until smooth. Gradually add the remaining flour, beating constantly, then add the yeast mixture. Beat with a spoon until mixture forms a large ball. Turn out the dough onto a floured board. Knead thoroughly for 10 minutes, or until it feels elastic and no longer sticks to your hands. Transfer dough to a large, greased bowl and cover lightly with a damp cloth. Let rise at room temperature for 1 hour (dough is rather dry, so it will not rise much).

Roll out dough on a floured board into an 8 x 10-inch rectangle. Spread poppyseed filling over the surface, leaving a margin of about ½ inch around the edges. Starting from the side farthest from you, roll dough toward you. When rolled, turn cake over so the seam is on the underside, and tuck the edges of the roll under on each side to prevent the filling from escaping. Carefully transfer the roll to cookie sheet and cover lightly with a damp kitchen towel. Let rise in a warm place for 1 hour.

Preheat the oven to 400°F. Uncover cake and place in oven. Bake for 10 minutes, then reduce the heat to 375°F, and bake for 30 minutes more, or until golden brown.

Remove the cake from the oven and let it cool completely before transferring to a wire rack. To make the frosting, sift the confectioners sugar into a bowl. Make a well in the center and fill with the egg white and lemon juice. Combine ingredients with a wooden spoon until the frosting is absolutely smooth, then spread frosting evenly over the top of the cake, letting it drip down the sides, or drizzle icing in a zigzag manner across top.

Cinnamon Streusel

This is an Austrian cake, served usually with coffee.

dairy

SERVES 8 TO 10

1 envelope active dry yeast	CRUMB TOPPING
½ cup sugar	1 cup all-purpose flour
½ cup lukewarm milk	2 teaspoons ground cinnamon
2 cups all-purpose flour	4 tablespoons sugar
¼ teaspoon salt	¼ cup butter, melted
½ cup butter, softened	
2 eggs	

In a bowl, mix the yeast with 1 teaspoon sugar, then add the milk. Stir and cover the mixture lightly with a cloth. Let rest in a warm place to proof for about 20 minutes.

Sift the flour and salt into a large bowl. Add the yeast mixture, half the butter, and the rest of the sugar. Beat well to form a dough, then knead dough on a floured board until it no longer sticks to your fingers and is elastic, about 10 minutes. Put dough in a greased bowl, cover with plastic wrap, and let rise until doubled in bulk, about 2 hours.

Punch dough down, then roll out to fit a greased standard jellyroll pan. Lay dough in the pan. Melt remaining butter and brush it over the dough; let dough rise in a warm place for 45 minutes.

Preheat oven to 350°F. Make the crumb topping by sifting the flour into a bowl. Add the cinnamon and sugar along with the melted butter. Blend until mixture resembles coarse breadcrumbs, then sprinkle crumbs over the dough. Bake the cake for 30 minutes, or until golden.

 Iced Poppyseed Roll; recipe on page 139

Lekach

This honey cake is traditional among all European Jews at New Year's. Honey cake has a bad habit of sticking to the pan, so grease and flour it well, or line it with nonstick baking paper. Photo opposite.

pareve

SERVES 12

3 tablespoons margarine, softened
4 eggs plus 1 egg yolk
1 cup sugar
1 cup honey
1 cup strong black coffee
3 cups sifted whole-wheat flour
1½ teaspoons baking powder

1 teaspoon baking soda
1 teaspoon ground cinnamon
½ teaspoon ground ginger
½ teaspoon ground allspice
1 cup coarsely chopped blanched almonds
6 almonds, blanched and halved
2 teaspoons water

Preheat the oven to 350°F. Grease and flour a 9 x 12-inch cake pan or line it with nonstick paper.

Beat the margarine in a bowl with the whole eggs and the sugar. Stir in the honey and coffee, and blend well. Sift the flour again with the baking powder, baking soda, and spices. Fold the dry ingredients into the egg mixture and beat well. Lastly add the chopped almonds, and mix well.

Pour the mixture into the pan and arrange the almond halves in rows on top. Lightly beat the egg yolk with the water and brush over the top of the cake. Bake the cake for 1 hour, or until the almonds are lightly browned and cake springs back when pushed gently with your finger. Cool cake completely in the pan before turning it out onto a wire rack.

Fluden

This delicious German jelly roll is very popular in Israel for late Friday evening, when the inevitable guests make their appearances. Use the thick, dark plum jam known in Polish as *powidla*.

pareve

SERVES 10

2 cups all-purpose flour
½ teaspoon salt
½ teaspoon baking powder
¾ cup shortening, cut in pieces
2 egg yolks, lightly beaten
2 oranges, juices squeezed and rinds grated

⅔ cup good plum jam
4 tablespoons confectioners sugar
2 tablespoons ground cinnamon
1 cup chopped walnuts
1 egg lightly beaten with 2 teaspoons water

Sift the flour, salt, and baking powder into the bowl of a food processor. Add the shortening and blend until mixture resembles coarse breadcrumbs. With the beaters running, pour in the egg yolks, orange juice, and rind and blend until mixture forms a ball of dough. Wrap dough in plastic and chill for at least 30 minutes.

Preheat oven to 350°F. Grease a large cookie sheet. Divide the dough in half. Roll out 1 piece of dough on a floured board into a large 8 x 12-inch rectangle. Briefly warm the jam, then spread half over the dough, leaving a ½-inch border around edge.

Combine the confectioners sugar, cinnamon, and nuts in a small bowl, then sprinkle half this mixture over the jam. Roll up dough like a jelly roll and lay it, seam side down, on the cookie sheet. Roll out the other piece of dough, spread it with the rest of the jam, and sprinkle with the rest of the nut mixture. Roll up as before and transfer to the cookie sheet alongside first roll. Brush both rolls with the beaten egg. Bake for 30 minutes, or until golden brown. Allow to cool completely before slicing.

Apple Strudel

Strudel is so inextricably linked with Jews in most people's minds that I have included it here. Jewish cooks did indeed bake strudel frequently in the days of the Austro-Hungarian Empire. My mother's friend Lisl Ullmann tells me her mother insisted the strudel dough had to be so thin you could read a newspaper through it! In fact, this paper-thin dough was introduced to the Austrians by their archenemies, the Turks.

There are many different possible fillings, including cottage cheese, sauerkraut, even liver, but apple filling is the most popular. Strudel dough is hard to make at home unless you have had lots of practice, but you can easily substitute phyllo dough from a Greek or Middle Eastern bakery. (For instructions on using phyllo dough, see the recipe for Bourekas, page 26.)

pareve

SERVES 8 TO 10

4 large sheets phyllo dough
4 tablespoons margarine, melted
1 cup matzo meal
1 cup ground almonds
6 large dessert apples, peeled, cored, and
   coarsely chopped

1 lemon, rind grated and juice squeezed
1 cup golden raisins
½ cup granulated sugar
2 tablespoons ground cinnamon
confectioners sugar to decorate

Preheat oven to 400°F. Lightly grease 2 large cookie sheets.

Lay a sheet of phyllo dough on a floured cloth. Brush it with melted margarine and lay another sheet on top. Brush this with melted margarine, also.

Combine remaining ingredients except confectioners sugar. Spread half the mixture evenly over the dough, up to ½ inch from edge. Roll up the dough like a jelly roll, using the cloth to help support the dough. Transfer roll to one of the cookie sheets. Repeat the procedure with the 2 remaining sheets of dough, melted margarine, and filling. Transfer this roll to other cookie sheet. Bake strudels for 40 minutes, or until well browned. Slice while warm and sprinkle with sifted confectioners sugar.

Ponchiki

These doughnuts were a specialty of Warsaw Jewish bakers. The Polish Catholics who stood in line to buy them in the depths of wir did not realize that they were eating a Jewish delicacy made Chanukah, when fried foods are traditional. Nowadays these d as popular in Israel, where even Arabs enjoy them.

dairy

SERVES 8 TO 10

2½ cups all-purpose flour
1 teaspoon baking powder
2 eggs
1½ cups sour cream
2 tablespoons granulated sugar

¼ teaspoon salt
½ teaspoon vanilla extract
oil for deep-frying
3 cups confectioners sugar

Combine all ingredients except oil and confectioners sugar in a large mixing bowl. Blend well; the batter will be very soft.

Heat the oil in a deep-fryer until it is so hot that a cube of bread dropped into it will brown in 1 minute, about 375°F. Drop a few table-spoons of the mixture carefully into the oil and fry until golden brown on one side, then turn and fry on other side, about 3 minutes. Drain on paper towels and continue with remaining batter. When all the doughnuts are done, pour the confectioners sugar onto a shallow platter and roll doughnuts in it to coat thoroughly. Serve warm.

✡

Taiglech

These fried cookies are eaten at New Year's. The name means "little pieces of dough," and although they are Eastern European, they quite obviously have Middle Eastern origins (see the recipe for Gushfil, page 147, and note the similarity).

pareve

MAKES 30

2 cups all-purpose flour
2 teaspoons ground ginger
¼ teaspoon salt

2 eggs, lightly beaten
2 cups clear honey

Sift the flour into a bowl along with half the ginger and the salt. Add the eggs, mix thoroughly, and knead to a smooth dough, adding a couple of tablespoons of water if the mixture is too dry to become smooth. Roll out dough onto a floured board and cut into 1-inch squares.

Rinse 2 cookie sheets under cold water. Heat the honey in a large saucepan over high heat with the remaining ginger but don't stir. When the honey boils, reduce heat and add a few pieces of dough, a few at a time. Boil them gently until they turn pale brown, about 20 minutes. Remove cookies with a slotted spoon and drain on the cookie sheets. Keep warm while you make remaining cookies. Serve warm.

Rugelach

Cookies made in crescent shapes were popular in Vienna, where they symbolized victory over the Turks. These Polish cookies are from Galicia, once part of the Austro-Hungarian Empire.

dairy

MAKES 64

2 cups all-purpose flour
1/4 teaspoon salt
1/2 teaspoon baking powder
1 cup sugar
1 cup butter, softened
8 ounces cream cheese, at room temperature

1 tablespoon ground cinnamon
1/2 cup golden raisins
1/2 cup chopped walnuts
1/2 cup warm milk mixed with 1 teaspoon sugar

Sift the flour, salt, and baking powder into a bowl. Add half the sugar and mix well. Add the butter and cream cheese and work it into the dough. Wrap dough in plastic and refrigerate for at least 2 hours.

Preheat oven to 375°F. Lightly grease a cookie sheet. Divide the dough into 8 balls. In a small bowl, combine the rest of the sugar with the cinnamon, raisins, and walnuts. Roll out a piece of dough into a 10-inch circle. With a sharp knife, cut the circle into 8 pie-shaped segments. Sprinkle some filling over the circle, then roll up each segment, starting from the wide end; when roll is completed, bend the ends so you have a crescent shape. Roll out, cut, and sprinkle remaining pieces of dough with filling. Roll and shape remaining segments into crescents. Arrange crescents on the cookie sheet and brush with the milk mixture. Bake for 20 minutes, or until golden brown. Let cool on a rack.

Gushfil

Persian Jews think big. While the Ashkenazim only make Haman's ears for Purim, the Persians make these elephants' ears! These cookies, from Rita Levy, formerly of Meshhed, are typical deep-fried cookies popular throughout western Asia.

pareve

MAKES 20

2 cups all-purpose flour
¼ teaspoon salt
1 egg, lightly beaten

2 cups oil
2 tablespoons water
2 cups honey or syrup

Sift the flour into a bowl along with the salt. Add the egg, 1 tablespoon of the oil, and the water, beating until dough is smooth. Knead dough until it no longer sticks to your fingers, about 10 minutes. Put dough into a plastic bag and refrigerate for 30 minutes.

Roll out dough as thin as possible on a floured board into a strip about 12 inches wide. Use a ravioli cutter, pastry wheel, or sharp knife to cut the dough lengthwise into 12 long strips.

Heat the remaining oil in a deep skillet until it starts to smoke, about 375°F. Loosely wind a strip of dough around your hand, like winding wool. Drop the dough strand into the hot oil and fry until golden, about 2 minutes. Remove and drain. Repeat with the remaining strips, draining on absorbent paper.

Heat the honey or syrup to boiling point, then remove from the heat. Dip the cooked pastries into the hot syrup and coat each thoroughly. Remove and pile on a plate. Eat immediately.

VARIATION

Instead of dipping the pastries in syrup, dredge them with confectioners sugar.

Hamantashen

These 3-cornered Purim cookies are called Haman's ears if they are small, and Haman's hats or pockets if they are big. The cookies are often in the small packages of candies and other delicacies that are exchanged at Purim.

Since canned poppyseed and prune fillings are readily available in supermarkets, I have suggested using them instead of preparing the filling from scratch. If you can get freshly ground poppyseed or can grind it yourself in a coffee grinder, make the filling from 1 cup ground poppyseed, 1 cup soft brown sugar, ½ cup margarine or butter, and 1 tablespoon brandy. For prune filling, use 2 cups chopped pitted prunes, ½ cup brown sugar or honey, ½ cup margarine or butter, and 1 tablespoon brandy. Cook either mixture in a saucepan over medium heat, stirring constantly until it comes to a boil. Simmer 5 minutes, then let cool.

Many people use a yeast dough for these cookies, however this dough is quicker and simpler.

dairy

MAKES 40 SMALL

2½ cups all-purpose flour	1 egg, lightly beaten
2½ teaspoons baking powder	¾ cup milk
1 teaspoon salt	1 can (12½ ounces) poppyseed or prune
½ cup sugar	filling
4 tablespoons margarine or butter, softened	1 egg yolk mixed with 2 teaspoons water

Preheat the oven to 350°F. Sift the flour, baking powder, and salt into a bowl and add the sugar. Cream the margarine or butter with the egg and milk, then add to the dry ingredients. Mix well.

Sprinkle a work surface with flour and knead the dough until it is smooth and elastic, about 5 minutes. Roll out dough to a thickness of ⅛ inch. Use a glass or cookie cutter to cut out 2-inch circles of dough. Place a teaspoon of filling in the center of each circle, then pinch the circles to form a triangle with a little filling showing through in the center. Brush the tops of the cookies with the egg-yolk mixture, then bake for 30 minutes or until the crust is golden brown. Cool on a rack.

Mandelbrod

These zweiback-style cookies, called *komishbrod*, were introduced into Eastern Europe from the south—probably from southern Italy, where an almost identical cookie, *biscotta alla mandorla*, is popular. It is equally possible, however, that the recipe spread from Spain, both to southern Italy, which was once under Spanish rule, and to the Netherlands, where a variation on this recipe is known as *spekulaasje*.

pareve

MAKES 40

2½ cups all-purpose flour
4 teaspoons baking powder
½ teaspoon salt
3 eggs
1 cup sugar

6 tablespoons oil
grated rind of 1 lemon
½ teaspoon almond extract
½ cup chopped or slivered almonds

Preheat the oven to 350°F. Flour a cookie sheet, but do not grease it.

Sift the flour, baking powder, and salt into a bowl. Beat the eggs and sugar together until pale and foaming, then add the oil, lemon rind, and almond extract. Fold the egg mixture into the dry ingredients and beat until the dough is smooth. Stir in the almonds.

Sprinkle your hands and a board with flour. Divide the dough in half and shape each half into a long loaf about 3 inches wide. Lay each loaf on the cookie sheet and bake until lightly browned, about 40 minutes.

Remove the loaves from the oven, and while they are still warm, use a sharp knife to cut ½-inch slices. Increase the oven temperature to 450°F, then arrange the slices on the cookie sheet and place back in oven. Brown slices for about 7 minutes on each side, or until toasted. Cool on a rack.

Jødekagar

These cookies are known as Jewish cakes in Denmark. My grandmother used to call them wine biscuits, because they are often served at Kiddush, the blessing over the wine.

pareve

MAKES 40

3 cups all-purpose flour
½ teaspoon salt
1 cup margarine
1 egg, lightly beaten
2 drops almond extract

1 cup sugar
1 egg beaten with 2 teaspoons water
1 tablespoon ground cinnamon
1 cup chopped almonds

Sift the flour and salt into a bowl. Rub the margarine into the flour with the fingertips until mixture resembles fine breadcrumbs. Stir in the beaten egg, almond extract, and ¾ cup of sugar. Knead just until the dough is smooth. Put dough in a plastic bag and refrigerate for 30 minutes.

Preheat the oven to 425°F. Lightly grease a cookie sheet.

Roll out dough to ½ inch thickness and cut it into shapes with cookie cutters (circles or stars). Arrange on cookie sheets and brush them with the egg-beaten mixture. Sprinkle cookies lightly with remaining sugar, the cinnamon, and the chopped nuts. Bake for about 5 minutes, or until lightly browned at the edges. Cool on a rack.

Mount Sinai Cakes

Sephardic Jews bake these cookies for Shavuot to celebrate Moses' receiving the commandments on Mount Sinai. Since dairy dishes are traditional on the Feast of Weeks, these cookies are made with butter; however, margarine can always be substituted to make the cookies pareve.

dairy

MAKES 40

2 cups all-purpose flour
½ teaspoon salt
1 teaspoon ground cinnamon
¼ teaspoon grated nutmeg
4 eggs, lightly beaten

½ cup soft brown sugar
6 tablespoons butter, melted
2 tablespoons brandy
about 40 walnut halves

Preheat oven to 350°F. Lightly grease 2 cookie sheets.

Sift the flour, salt, cinnamon, and nutmeg into a bowl. In another bowl, beat the eggs, sugar, butter, and brandy until smooth. Add this mixture gradually to the flour mixture, beating well.

Break the dough into 1-inch balls. Mold the balls into cone shapes that resemble mountain peaks. Arrange peaks on cookie sheets. Stick a walnut half on top of each "peak." Bake cookies for 15 minutes, or until golden brown. Cool on a rack.

Passover Cinnamon Cookies

In our family the children baked the Passover cookies—well before preparations got under way for the main meal, of course. These cookies are very simple, but so delicious it is surprising they are not better known.

The stiffness of the cookie dough will depend on the amount of egg white used. If you find your dough is too soft to roll into balls, add a little more ground almonds.

pareve, kosher for Passover

MAKES 20

1 cup ground almonds	*2 egg whites*
1½ tablespoons ground cinnamon	*1 cup confectioners sugar*
1 cup granulated sugar	

Preheat the oven to 350°F. Grease a cookie sheet.

Put the ground almonds, cinnamon, and sugar into a bowl, and mix thoroughly. In another bowl, beat the egg whites until stiff, then fold them into the dry ingredients.

Wet your hands and shape the mixture into small balls the size of a large walnut. Arrange on the cookie sheet (you can put them quite close together; they do not swell while cooking), and bake for 25 minutes.

Put the confectioners sugar in a shallow bowl, then roll the baked cookies in the sugar until thickly coated. Set to cool on a rack.

Stuffed Monkey

This delicious Sephardic cake is popular among English Jews, though the meaning of the name is unknown. One theory is that *monkey* is a corruption of *machshee*, Arabic for "stuffed" or "filled."

pareve

SERVES 10

1 egg white, beaten with 2 teaspoons
   water
1 cup slivered almonds

DOUGH
2 cups all-purpose flour
½ teaspoon salt
1 teaspoon ground cinnamon
½ cup margarine
½ cup brown sugar
1 egg, lightly beaten
3 drops almond extract

FILLING
½ cup chopped candied peel
½ cup chopped nuts (almonds, pecans,
   cashews, or walnuts)
½ cup golden raisins
½ teaspoon ground cinnamon
½ teaspoon ground allspice
2 tablespoons sugar
1 egg yolk
3 tablespoons margarine, melted

Make the dough. Sift the flour, salt, and cinnamon into a bowl and rub in the margarine until mixture resembles breadcrumbs. Stir in the beaten egg to bind, and add the almond extract. If the dough is too stiff to form into a ball, add a tablespoon or 2 of water. Knead dough until smooth, then divide in half. Wrap each half in plastic and refrigerate for at least 20 minutes.

Preheat oven to 375°F. Lightly grease a 9 x 14-inch jellyroll pan.

To make the filling, combine ingredients in a bowl and mix well.

Roll out 1 piece of dough on a floured board to fit the jellyroll pan. Spread filling over the dough, then roll out the other piece of dough and lay it over the filling. Pinch edges together so the filling does not leak out. Brush top of dough with the egg white mixture and generously sprinkle with the almonds. Bake for 30 minutes, or until golden-brown. Cut into bars to serve.

CHAPTER

11

BREADS

This is a small chapter, because most Jewish breads are store-bought. Always remember these simple rules when making yeast doughs: Every utensil should be warmed, follow the package directions for the yeast even if it conflicts with the recipe directions, and never work in a draft. Yeast is a live organism, so treat it with respect.

Challah

This braided loaf for the Sabbath and festivals is common among Ashkenazic, Italian, and "true" Sephardic communities. Only the Middle Eastern, North African, and Persian Jews do not have a braided bread for Sabbath and festivals.

Challahs are often braided in a complex way, but a simple 3-strand braid is used here. A specially big challah shaped with several braids of different sizes is baked for a wedding, bar mitzvah, or other celebration; it is sugar-glazed and decorated with sprinkles. A round challah, made from a strip of dough wound into a snail shape, is traditional on the New Year to symbolize the continuing cycle of the years. Normally, 2 challah are baked at once and put on the Friday night table, covered with a cloth until the meal is about to start.

When baking challah containing more than 3 pounds of flour, break off a tiny piece of dough about the size of a walnut. Recite a blessing and burn the piece (formerly it was thrown into the fire). This is to symbolize the portion of bread that was given to the priests when the Temple stood in Jerusalem.

pareve

MAKES 2 LOAVES

1 envelope active dry yeast or ½ cake compressed yeast	1 teaspoon salt
1 teaspoon sugar	2 tablespoons oil
2 cups warm water	1 egg, at room temperature
8 cups all-purpose flour	1 egg beaten with 2 teaspoons water
	4 tablespoons poppyseeds or sesame seeds

In a small bowl, combine the yeast with the sugar and ½ cup water. Cover with plastic and leave in a warm place until well-risen, about 20 minutes.

Sift the flour and salt into a warmed bowl. Make a well in the center and break the egg into it. Add the yeast mixture and stir with a wooden spoon, gradually incorporating the liquid into the flour. Gradually add enough remaining warm water to make a stiff dough. Turn the dough onto a floured board and knead until it is smooth and elastic, and it doesn't stick to your hands, about 10 minutes. Put dough in a warmed, greased bowl. Cover it with plastic, and let rise until doubled, about 2 hours.

Punch down the dough and divide into 6 balls. Roll the balls between your hands into long strips of equal length and about 1 inch wide. Braid 3 strips together and place on greased cookie sheet. Wrap the ends neatly underneath the loaf. Repeat with the remaining 3 strips to make another loaf. Cover the loaves with a kitchen towel and leave them in a warm place to rise for about 45 minutes. (Alternatively, put them in large plastic bags and leave them in the refrigerator overnight. Then let them rise the next day.)

Preheat the oven to 450°F. Brush the loaves with the beaten egg-and-water mixture and sprinkle with the seeds. Bake loaves for 15 minutes, then reduce the heat to 375°F and bake for 40 minutes, or until golden brown. Let cool on a rack.

Jewish Corn Bread

This is a very confusing name, because there is no corn in this rye bread. The confusion arises because the German and Yiddish name for wheat is *korn*. Actually the bread is half-wheat, half-rye flour. Rye is a difficult flour for bread-making because it has very little gluten and rises only minimally. It is a good idea to leave the loaves in a cool place overnight to rise.

pareve

MAKES 2 LOAVES

1 tablespoon molasses	1/2 cup warm water
1 ounce unsweetened chocolate	4 cups medium rye flour
3 tablespoons margarine	2 cups all-purpose flour
1 cup water	1/2 cup semolina
1 teaspoon salt	1 egg white mixed with 2 teaspoons
1 envelope active dry yeast or 1/2 cake	water
compressed yeast	

In a small pan, heat the molasses, chocolate, 1 tablespoon margarine, and water until chocolate melts and mixture is dissolved. Let cool to lukewarm.

Dissolve the yeast in ½ cup warm water, then add it to the molasses mixture. Sift the flours into a large bowl and mix well. Gradually beat in the liquid until the dough is smooth, then turn out onto a floured work surface and knead until smooth, about 10 minutes. A rye loaf will not be as smooth and elastic as a wheat loaf, so take care not to overknead. Put the dough in a greased bowl, cover with plastic, and let rise until doubled in bulk, about 3 hours (or overnight in a cool place).

Shape the dough into 2 round loaves. Sprinkle a large cookie sheet with semolina and transfer the loaves to the sheet. Cover with a damp kitchen towel, and let rise in a warm place for 1 hour.

Preheat oven to 425°F. Brush loaves with the egg-white-and-water mixture. Bake for 30 minutes, then reduce the heat and bake at 400°F for another 20 minutes or until done. To test for doneness, rap a loaf on the bottom with your knuckles; if it sounds hollow, it is ready. Let cool on a rack.

Bagels

Once described as tasting "like a doughnut dipped in cement," these rolls were invented by a Polish Jewish baker to celebrate the victory of his King, Jan Sobieski, in the Siege of Vienna, 1683. Originally they were to be in the shape of a stirrup (German word for a stirrup is *beugel*). Successfully transplanted to the other side of the world by Jewish bakers, bagels were, like knishes, once confined to the Lower East Side of New York. Now bagel bakeries have sprung up all over the United States, as bagel fever spreads. Everyone can appreciate how delicious a bagel is, especially topped with cream cheese and lox (smoked salmon).

Bagels vary from community to community, in different parts of the world. The high-rising, commercial American bagel is made with high-gluten flour, and is far less tasty than the thinner and crustier European and Israeli versions. The following recipe is for the latter variety. If you like egg bagels (which are an American invention), add an egg to the mixture along with the water.

pareve

MAKES 20

1 envelope active dry yeast or ½ cake
   compressed yeast
2 tablespoons sugar
1 teaspoon salt

¼ cup margarine
1 cup water
4 cups all-purpose flour

Mix the yeast with 1 tablespoon of sugar. Put the remaining sugar, salt, margarine, and water in a saucepan and heat over low heat until the margarine melts. Let cool to lukewarm.

Sift the flour into a large bowl and gradually stir in the liquid. When the dough is smooth, turn out onto a floured board and knead until it no longer sticks to your fingers, about 10 minutes. Put dough into a warmed, greased bowl and cover with plastic. Leave it in a warm place to rise until doubled in bulk, about 2 hours.

Punch dough down, then divide into 20 balls of equal size. Roll each ball into a strip about 5 inches long and shape the strip into a ring, pinching the ends very firmly together so they do not come apart during cooking. Arrange the rings on a floured board and cover with a damp cloth. Leave them in a warm place to rise for 45 minutes.

Bring a large pan of water to a boil over high heat. Reduce the heat and when the water is boiling very gently, drop a ring into it. As soon as it rises to the top, remove it with a skimmer. Drain on a wooden board or absorbent paper and repeat with the rest of the rings.

Preheat oven to 400°F. Grease 2 cookie sheets. Transfer the rings to the cookie sheets and bake until crisp and golden brown, about 30 minutes. Cool on wire racks.

VARIATION:
To make bagel zwiebacks, slice day-old bagels into thin pieces, then toast in a very cool oven. Store in an airtight container.

Bialystoker Rolls

Bialys are almost as popular as bagels; I think the bialys sold in London's East End are the most delicious. The name comes from the city of Bialystok, once in Poland, now part of the Soviet Union.

pareve

MAKES 20

1 envelope active dry yeast
1 cup lukewarm water
2 teaspoons sugar
4 cups all-purpose flour

½ teaspoon salt
1 egg beaten with 2 teaspoons water
2 onions

Dissolve the yeast in the water and add the sugar. Let rise in a warm place, lightly covered, until it foams, about 20 minutes.

Sift the flour and salt into a large bowl. Add the yeast mixture and work into a dough. Put the dough into a greased bowl, cover with a damp cloth, and let rise until doubled in bulk, about 1½ hours.

Punch dough down and divide into 20 pieces. On a floured board, shape each into a round roll, then transfer the rolls to 2 floured cookie sheets. Cover lightly with a cloth and let rise for 45 minutes.

Preheat oven to 400°F. Chop the onions. Press your thumb into the center of each roll to make a shallow depression. Brush depression with the beaten egg mixture, and sprinkle with some chopped onion. Sprinkle very lightly with flour. Bake rolls for 20 minutes, or until golden. Cool on wire racks. Serve split and buttered.

Polish Potato Bread

This robust bread is typical of Galicia, the part of the Austro-Hungarian Empire that is now Poland. The low-lying, marsh land is very suitable for potato-growing, and, like Ireland, supported the impoverished population for many years.

pareve

MAKES 2 LOAVES

1 envelope active dry yeast
1 teaspoon sugar
¼ cup lukewarm water
1 large onion, chopped
2 tablespoons oil

2 cups all-purpose flour
1 teaspoon salt
6 large potatoes
½ teaspoon black pepper
3 eggs, lightly beaten

Dissolve the yeast and sugar in the warm water and leave in a warm place, lightly covered, until the mixture foams, about 20 minutes.

Sauté the onion in the oil until transparent, about 5 minutes. Let cool.

Sift the flour, salt, and pepper into a large bowl. Peel and grate the potatoes, saving any liquid, then add potatoes and potato liquid to the flour immediately, before the potatoes start to blacken. Add the yeast mixture, eggs, and fried onion, and mix to a smooth dough. Knead the dough well on a floured board until it no longer sticks to your fingers or the board, about 10 minutes. Put dough into a greased bowl and cover the bowl with plastic. Leave in a warm place until doubled in bulk, about 2 hours.

Preheat oven to 375°F. Grease two 1-quart loaf pans and divide the dough between them. Let rise again until doubled, about 45 minutes. Bake the loaves 45 minutes, or until golden brown. Let cool briefly, then serve warm.

Pita Bread

Believe it or not, pita is a Hebrew word. This bread has been changed in various countries and has even been modified into pizza! Pita is traditionally made from white flour, although whole-wheat pitas are also sold.

In Israel, there are 2 types of pita, the puffy kind you find in the United States, and a flatbread similar to Armenian *lavash*. The latter is baked in a large barrel-shaped oven, in which the fire is at the bottom of a pit and the dough is slapped against the walls for a few seconds to cook. To get the same effect, bake the pita on a very hot griddle or in a dry red-hot skillet.

pareve

MAKES 25

1 envelope active dry yeast	4 cups all-purpose flour
1 teaspoon sugar	½ teaspoon salt
1½ cups lukewarm water	

Combine the yeast and sugar in a bowl with half the water, and leave in a warm place, lightly covered, until the yeast foams, about 20 minutes.

Sift the flour and salt into a bowl and gradually add the yeast mixture. Stir with a wooden spoon while adding the rest of the water to form a stiff dough. Knead the dough until it is smooth and elastic and no longer sticks to the bowl or your fingers, about 10 minutes. Divide dough into 25 equal-size pieces and let pieces rest in a warm place for 30 minutes.

Roll out each piece of dough on a floured board to form a thin round. Sprinkle lightly with more flour and let rise for 1 hour.

Flatten rounds and roll out again. Let them rise for another 30 minutes.

Preheat oven to 500°F. Bake in batches, each about 10 minutes; they will puff up but will flatten immediately when removed from oven. They should only be allowed to brown slightly.

HINT

Never throw away stale pita (unless it has gone moldy). Sprinkle it with water and cut it into strips, then bake it for 15 minutes in a very cool oven, about 300°F. It will then be crisp as zwieback, and can be used in the same way. Incidentally, pita is especially delicious for dipping in a fondue because it is all crust.

Kubaneh

This is a Yemenite sweet bread eaten on the Sabbath. Originally, Kubaneh contained only a little sugar to help the yeast work, but since they came to Israel, Yemenites have had access to cheap sugar and have sweetened the recipe accordingly. This recipe produces a soft, semi-steamed bread. Eat it with melted margarine and jelly, jam, or preserves.

pareve

SERVES 8

1 envelope active dry yeast
3 cups lukewarm water
½ cup sugar

4 cups all-purpose flour
¼ teaspoon salt
½ teaspoon ground ginger

Dissolve the yeast in 1 cup of the water, along with 1 teaspoon of the sugar. Lightly cover with a cloth and leave in a warm place until the yeast foams, about 20 minutes.

Sift the flour into a large bowl and add the salt, ginger, and remaining sugar. Pour the yeast mixture into the flour, then beat in the rest of the water. Stir the mixture until it forms a soft dough. Turn out onto a floured board and knead well until the dough is elastic, about 10 minutes. Cover lightly and let rise until doubled in bulk, about 2 hours.

Shape the dough into a thick rope. Grease a deep 10-inch tube pan and fill it with the dough. Cover lightly and let rise until doubled in bulk, about 45 minutes.

Preheat oven to 350°F. Grease a sheet of aluminum foil and cover the tube pan with it. Bake bread for 1½ hours, or lower heat to 250°F and bake overnight as you would a cholent. Pierce the foil with a fork to release steam, then remove carefully so as not burn yourself. Turn the bread out onto a wire rack to cool.

12

DRINKS

Not many drinks can be said to be specifically Jewish, however wine is very important in Jewish ritual. In Moslem countries, where alcohol is forbidden, Jews often make their own alcoholic brews. For instance, Tunisian Jews produce a liqueur called *bouha* from figs.

There are some drinks that have been brought by Jews from their countries of origin, which have become popular among other communities. For instance, fruit syrups diluted with hot water, such as hot black currant and hot lemon, have become popular winter drinks in northern England where Jews have settled, such as in Leeds and Gateshead.

Kefir

This thin yogurt drink is wonderfully refreshing in the summer. It was introduced into Russia by the Tartars, and is now drunk all over Asia, Turkey, and the Soviet Union.

dairy, kosher for Passover

SERVES 4

2 cups thick plain yogurt
2 cups cold water
½ teaspoon salt

1 cup crushed ice
fresh mint sprigs or dried mint

Put the yogurt in a blender. Add the water and salt and blend until smooth. Pour into 4 tall glasses and top with crushed ice. Place a sprig of mint on each glass or crumble on a little dried mint. Drink through straws.

Russian Tea

This is best made in a samovar, but you can devise a pretty good substitute. A samovar is just an urn containing hot water. The top part holds a large quantity of water, poured in from a lid in the top. At the bottom is a faucet to pour the water out. Just below the urn are charcoals to heat the contents. On top of the samovar sits a tiny metal teapot with a very strong brew of tea. Any kind of tea can be used; Russian tea is grown in the Soviet Republic of Georgia and tastes like a cross between Indian and China teas.

pareve, kosher for Passover

MAKES 10 TO 12 CUPS

4 teaspoons tea leaves
freshly boiled water

1 lemon, sliced
sugar or preserves

Place a small metal teapot near a large tea kettle. Bring the kettle of water almost to a boil, but stop it before it boils. Pour a little water into the pot, swill it round, and pour it out so the pot is warmed. Add the tea leaves to the pot.

Bring the water in the kettle to a full boil (the steam will pour out in a straight line) and immediately pour it into the teapot. Put the pot in a warm place and let the tea brew for at least 15 minutes.

Put a teaspoon into a tall glass with a holder. Pour about 2 tablespoons of brewed tea into the glass, then top off the glass with freshly boiled water. The tea should be a rich amber color. Add a slice of lemon.

Western Russians sweeten their tea by placing a sugar cube between their teeth and drinking the tea through the sugar. This is not good dental practice, and is not recommended. Eastern Russians eat preserves with the tea to sweeten it.

When the tea from the little teapot is finished, make a fresh brew; *never* add more boiling water to used tea leaves, or else the tea will be bitter and weak.

Israeli-Style Coffee

So-called Turkish coffee is made and served differently in each country. In Israel, both Jews and town-dwelling Arabs brew their coffee in open pots with a wide rim—pots the Israelis call *finjan*, though this word simply means *cup* in Arabic. The Bedouins roast and grind their own coffee and serve it plain. Town-dwelling Arabs grind their coffee with cardamom seeds, so that it has a gloriously perfumed aroma. Israelis simply drop a whole cardamom pod into each tiny cup, or add a couple of pods to the pot.

To make Turkish-style coffee, grind the coffee beans to a fine powder. This can be done for you, or you can take ready-ground coffee and grind it again in your own machine. The best coffee for this is dark roasted and comes from the Arabian peninsula. You could do what many Israelis do, and simply pour boiling water over a spoonful of finely ground coffee, as if it were the instant variety. This leaves a thick sludge in the bottom of the cup or glass once the grounds have settled. It is therefore no surprise to learn that Israelis call this *kaffay bots*, "mud coffee."

Here is the longer but more satisfying method. Use a Middle Eastern coffeepot, which can be bought at specialty stores, because the shape helps to trap the steam and makes the grounds drop to the bottom. If you take sugar, you cannot add it later and stir; it must be added during the brewing. Vary the sugar to taste, or use none, like the Bedouin.

pareve, kosher for Passover

SERVES 4

4 green or white cardamom pods
1½ cups water

4 heaping teaspoons finely ground Turkish-style coffee
4 teaspoons sugar (optional)

Have tiny cups ready, and put a cardamom pod in each one. Pour the water into the coffeepot. Spoon the coffee and sugar, if using, onto the surface of the water and do not stir, but let it sink down naturally. Put the coffeepot over medium heat, holding it by its long handle and watching it constantly. The coffee will foam and start to boil over. As soon as the foam rises, remove the pot from the heat until the liquid drops down. Return it to the heat until it rises again. Repeat twice more. Pour into the cups, distributing the foam (which is a delicacy) as evenly as possible. Serve immediately.

Passover Coffee

Spring is an uncertain season, and if Passover is early, a comforting drink for cold mornings is welcome. In my family, this was the only time of year we took milk in our coffee. And crumbling the matzos into the coffee somehow makes all the difference.

dairy, kosher for Passover

SERVES 4

4 teaspoons instant coffee
4 cups milk
pinch of ground cinnamon

about 4 teaspoons sugar
2 matzos

Put a teaspoon of coffee into each of 4 mugs. Heat the milk, cinnamon, and sugar over medium heat until it comes to a boil. While the milk is heating, break the matzos into small pieces.

Pour the hot milk into the mugs, stir, and add as many pieces of matzo as will fit into the mugs without the milk overflowing. Drink hot with a spoon.

Gogl-Mogl

Another hot winter drink, popular in Austria and Hungary, but with much more kick than milky coffee! I learned to make gogl-mogl from the late Myriam Sela, who headed the Yugoslav section of the Israel Foreign Ministry, though she was from Vienna and was an Auschwitz survivor.

dairy, kosher for Passover

SERVES 4

2 eggs
4 cups milk
1 teaspoon vanilla extract

4 tablespoons sugar
½ cup brandy
pinch of grated nutmeg

In a saucepan, add all the ingredients in the order given except the nutmeg. Beat constantly over medium heat, using a wire whisk (hoop-shaped, with a wire coiled round). Reduce heat and continue to beat, whisking constantly until the mixture is very frothy. Serve immediately, sprinkled with a pinch of grated nutmeg.

Dried Lime Drink

This is a favorite with Jews from Basra in Iraq as well as Iranian Jews. Dried limes can be bought from Middle Eastern grocers, but you can also make your own by taking fresh limes and drying them slowly in a warm place, such as over a radiator. When the skins are tough, leathery, and yellow-brown, the limes are ready. They can be stored indefinitely in an airtight tin but should not be refrigerated.

pareve, kosher for Passover

SERVES 4

4 dried limes
4 cups water

sugar

Crush the limes roughly with an upended rolling pin or in a mortar with a pestle. Put them in a pan with the water, cover, and bring to a boil over high heat. Reduce heat and simmer 10 minutes. Strain into glasses and add sugar to taste. Serve immediately.

Raisin Wine

The Jews of Russia and Poland in particular are fond of home brewing. I once had dinner in a Polish home in Tel Aviv, where the master of the house proudly produced a whole range of flavored vodkas he had distilled himself; some of them, he assured me, were 110 proof!

Raisin wine is a popular brew for Passover. To make it you will need a large stone crock or glass jar that holds at least 3 quarts, some cheesecloth, about 4 bottles, and 4 corks. When making wine, always sterilize all utensils.

pareve, kosher for Passover

MAKES 2 QUARTS

1 pound seedless raisins	1 lemon
1 stick cinnamon	6 cups boiling water
2 cups sugar lumps	

Chop the raisins or grind them in a food processor. Put them into the crock along with the cinnamon stick and sugar lumps. Slice the lemon, removing any seeds, and add to the jar. Pour boiling water over the contents of the crock and stir until the sugar dissolves.

Cover the crock with cheesecloth. Keep in a cool, dark place and stir once a day for 1 week. Strain the wine through cheesecloth, then bottle and cork it. Keep bottles in a cool, dark place for at least 3 weeks before drinking. Keeps indefinitely.

13

CANDY

Homemade candies are traditional on Purim and Passover. Most other candy is now storebought but, as with other foods, Jews have been instrumental in popularizing their favorite candies. My Great-grandmother Amelia (Millie) was born in Holland, and had a passion for the hard little brown taffies called *hopjes*. My Grandma Dora inherited her passion, so she always had some *hopjes* on hand, and I knew where to find the candy in her apartment almost before I could walk!

Making candy is easy. You will need a heavy-based pan. The ideal pan is a solid, unlined copper basin which is also good for making jelly and preserves. Such a pan is expensive, but if you make a lot of candy and preserves it is worth buying, as your sugar will never burn. A candy thermometer—a very inexpensive item—is also essential for some candies. Finally, and most important, when sugar is boiled to very high temperatures, it can be dangerous; if it falls on your skin it will stick to it, so be very careful not to spill any. Keep small children out of the kitchen when making boiled candies. Do not refrigerate candies, as they will pick up moisture from the air in the refrigerator and go soggy. Store them in airtight containers, such as cookie tins or jars.

Ingber

This Passover carrot candy is popular in all Ashkenazic communities. *Ingber* means "ginger" in Yiddish.

pareve, kosher for Passover
MAKES 1 POUND

1 pound carrots	½ cup chopped walnuts or pecans
2 cups sugar	¼ teaspoon ground ginger

Peel the carrots, then grate them on a fine grater. Put the grated carrots and the sugar in a heavy pan, placed on a low heat. Stir the contents until the sugar has dissolved, then reduce the heat even further by putting an asbestos mat under the pot.

Rinse an 8 x 12-inch jellyroll pan or nonstick griddle pan under running water and keep it damp.

Continue to cook the carrots, stirring frequently, until the mixture is very thick, about 10 minutes. Test the mixture by dropping a little into a cup of cold water; if it sets hard as it touches the water, candy is ready.

Remove the pan from the heat and immediately stir in the nuts and ginger. Pour the mixture quickly onto the damp surface of the jellyroll or griddle pan. Let candy cool until it starts to set, then score 1-inch squares with a knife. Let cool completely. When the candy is cold, break it along the score lines.

Coconut Ice

Coconut ice was also a favorite because, like most homemade Jewish candies, it is kosher for Passover. Of course, there is no special reason to color half the coconut ice pink; use any color you like.

pareve, kosher for Passover
MAKES 48

1¼ cups water	2 cups shredded coconut
4 cups sugar	½ teaspoon vanilla extract
½ teaspoon cream of tartar	red coloring

Rinse an 8 x 12-inch jellyroll pan with cold water, then drain off excess. Put the water, sugar, and cream of tartar in a heavy-based pan. Bring to a boil over high heat without stirring, then reduce heat and boil gently for 12 minutes.

Have a large bowl ready. Carefully pour the syrup into the bowl and beat with a wooden spoon until it becomes cloudy. Beat in the coconut and vanilla extract. Pour half the mixture into the dampened jellyroll pan and then quickly stir a few drops of red coloring into the mixture remaining in the bowl. Pour pink mixture over the coconut mixture in the pan. As soon as the candy is firm, divide into 2 x 1-inch bars.

Passover Nut Candy

The Ashkenazic Jews call this *nuent* and use ground walnuts; Middle Eastern Jews call it *louzina* and make it with ground almonds.

pareve, kosher for Passover

MAKES 48

2 cups honey
½ cup sugar

6 cups ground blanched almonds or
    walnuts
halved walnuts or almonds for decoration

Rinse an 8 x 12-inch jellyroll pan with cold water; keep damp. In a heavy-based pan, bring the honey and sugar to a boil over high heat, then boil without stirring for 10 minutes.

Slowly add the nuts and stir in well. Cook until the syrup registers 238°F on a candy thermometer, then turn the mixture into the dampened pan. As it cools, cut diagonally into diamond shapes, using a sharp knife dipped in cold water. Decorate each diamond with a walnut or almond half.

Matzo Farfel Candy

This Passover candy can also be made at other times of the year using ordinary farfel.

pareve, kosher for Passover

MAKES ABOUT 45

2 cups honey

½ cup sugar

1 cup Matzo Farfel (recipe page 53)

3 cups chopped peanuts

Dampen an 8 x 12-inch jellyroll pan with cold water. Put the honey and sugar in a heavy-based pan and bring to a boil over high heat. Boil without stirring for 20 minutes, or until a candy thermometer registers 238°F.

Stir in the farfel and nuts, then turn the mixture into the jellyroll pan. As it cools, cut into diamond shapes with a sharp knife dipped in cold water. Let cool completely.

Poppyseed Candy

This is traditional on Purim in Eastern and Central Europe, where all kinds of poppyseed goodies are eaten.

pareve, kosher for Passover

MAKES ABOUT 1 POUND

1 cup honey

1 cup ground poppyseeds

½ cup ground almonds

½ teaspoon ground cinnamon

rice paper (optional)

Put all the ingredients in a heavy-based pan set over high heat, and stir well. Boil without stirring until the mixture is thick, about 10 minutes.

Cover a cookie sheet with rice paper or nonstick baking paper. Pour the mixture onto the sheet and use a wooden spoon dipped in oil to spread mixture evenly. Let cool to lukewarm, then mark it in squares. When cold, cut into ½-inch squares and remove the nonstick baking paper, if used. The rice paper can be eaten with the candy.

Semolina Candy

This Tunisian candy is another Purim treat.

pareve, kosher for Passover

MAKES ABOUT 25

2 cups semolina
¼ teaspoon salt
½ teaspoon ground cinnamon
2 eggs, lightly beaten
½ cup water
½ cup broken or coarsely chopped
    walnuts

½ cup confectioners sugar
rosewater
1 cup oil
1 cup clear honey

In a bowl, combine the semolina, salt, cinnamon, beaten eggs, and water. Knead to form a firm dough, then roll out dough as thinly as possible—about ¹⁄₁₆ inch—on a floured board. Use a ravioli cutter or sharp knife to slice the dough into 1-inch squares.

Grind the nuts and confectioners sugar together in a food processor or blender until a fine powder. Pile a teaspoonful of the mixture into the center of each semolina square. Fold each corner of the semolina square toward the center. Dip your fingers in rosewater to moisten and seal the edges of the dough.

Heat the oil in a deep skillet and fry a few of the semolina candies at a time until golden. Drain thoroughly on absorbent paper.

Warm the honey until it is a liquid. Arrange the candies on a serving dish and pour honey over them. Sprinkle with more rosewater.

Pomerantzen

Pomerantzen is the Yiddish word for "oranges," and it is derived from the French *pomme d'orange*. Jews were responsible for introducing citrus fruits into northern Europe, through their trade in the etrog, the fruit used for Sukkot. Any thick-skinned citrus peels can be used. Make an attractive curled shape by stringing the peels on a thread before soaking them in brine, parboiling, and dipping in syrup.

pareve, kosher for Passover

MAKES 6 CUPS

peels of 6 oranges or 6 small grapefruit   about 4 cups sugar
3 quarts water   confectioners sugar
1 tablespoon salt

Peel the fruit, removing as much of the white pith as possible. Slice peel into strips about 3 inches long and ½ inch wide. Let them curl up. Put peels in a large crock and add water and salt. Leave overnight.

Drain the peels and rinse thoroughly. Put in a saucepan of cold water and bring to a boil. Immediately after the water boils, drain the peels. Repeat this procedure 3 times. Weigh the peels.

Put an equal weight of sugar into a heavy-based pan (about 3 cups), then add half that amount of water (about 1½ cups) and bring to a boil without stirring. As soon as the syrup boils, add the peels and reduce the heat to low. Cook without stirring until all the syrup has been absorbed. Remove the peels, separate with a fork, and drain on wire racks with waxed paper beneath to catch the drips. When peels are cool enough to handle, pour 1 cup sugar into a shallow bowl and roll the peels in it, adding more sugar if necessary.

Spread out the peels again on racks and let dry, lightly covered with parchment or waxed paper, in a warm place for 2 days. Roll again, this time in confectioners sugar, then store in airtight tins.

Sumsum

These sesame seed candies will be familiar to anyone from Charleston. Just as the African slaves brought sesame seeds (*benne*) to the South, so Jews carried these nutritious seeds to Eastern Europe when they fled from persecution in Spain. The candies are very popular in Israel, where they are sold mainly at the kiosks–little booths selling drinks and snacks.

pareve, kosher for Passover

MAKES ABOUT 40

1 cup honey	⅓ cup water
1 cup sugar	2 cups sesame seeds

Have ready an oiled jellyroll pan. Pour the honey, sugar, and water into a heavy-based pan. Bring to a boil without stirring and boil until a candy thermometer registers 236°F, or until a drop of the syrup forms a soft ball in a glass of cold water.

Add the sesame seeds and cook until seeds start to darken. Remove from the heat immediately, and run the cold faucet over the base of the pan to stop the cooking process or you might burn the seeds. Turn the mixture into the jellyroll pan and smooth it with a knife dipped in cold water. Score candy into diamond shapes and cut apart as soon as it hardens.

14

PICKLES AND PRESERVES

Pickles and preserves are widely used in Jewish cooking and are to be found on every Jewish table. They are economical, and before refrigeration they were the only way of enjoying seasonal foods all year round. Jews enjoy a particularly wide variety of pickled fish and vegetables, and I have included some recipes for a few of them.

Dill Pickles

These are especially associated with Jewish cooking, even in Eastern Europe where they originate. Of course there are lots of versions, including some with plain salt, vinegar and salt, or various flavorings. This is a delicious yet simple recipe. The spices and herbs can be varied, but use at least 4 tablespoons of salt for every 3 cups of water.

pareve, kosher for Passover

MAKES 4 QUARTS

*3 pounds small pickling cucumbers,
  washed well*
8 cloves garlic, unpeeled
1 teaspoon dill seed
4 white peppercorns

4 whole coriander seeds
4 sprigs fresh dill
7 tablespoons coarse (kosher) salt
3½ cups warm water
1 cup white wine vinegar

Have ready four 1-quart commercial canning jars with rings and new lids. Wash the jars, rings, and lids thoroughly and put them in a water bath to sterilize while you prepare the pickles.

Mix the cucumbers, garlic, spices, and dill sprigs in a large bowl. In another bowl, mix the salt, water, and vinegar.

Remove the jars from the bath, and pack the cucumbers and spices into them as tightly as possible. Pour in liquid leaving ½ inch air space at the top. Stir and poke mixture with a wooden spoon handle to make sure there are no air bubbles in the jar. If one of the jars is only part full, mix up a little more pickling liquid and add it to the jar. Seal the jars.

Process the pickles in a water bath. Bring the water to a boil and boil 30 minutes. Let cool, then check seals. Leave pickles at room temperature for at least a week (longer if possible) before opening. They will keep indefinitely. Refrigerate when opened; they will keep 1 week.

Pickled Lemons

Pickled lemons are popular in North Africa, even though lemons are home-grown and available year round. Some are pickled sweet-and-sour, with sugar, vinegar, salt, and cinnamon. Others are sweet, not suitable for cooking with meat but meant to be eaten like candy.

The following recipe is at least 800 years old; it appears in a book written at the end of the 12th century C.E. by Saladin's personal physician. Choose juicy, glossy, unblemished lemons. The rinds are delicious when cooked with lamb or chicken, such as in Chicken with Olives (page 102).

pareve, kosher for Passover

MAKES 2 QUARTS

1 cup coarse (kosher) salt	10 allspice berries
8 lemons	10 coriander seeds
2 bay leaves	

Sprinkle 2 or 3 tablespoons of salt into each 1-quart commercial canning jar. Make 4 lengthwise cuts in the lemons, from the end opposite the stem almost to the stem, but leave them joined at the stem end. Open up the cuts and pack them with coarse salt. Squeeze the lemons back into shape.

Pack lemons tightly into the jars, pushing them down firmly so they release their juices. Sprinkle with extra salt, and push the bay leaves down between the lemons; add the allspice berries and coriander seeds. Squeeze the remaining lemons and strain the juice. Pour juice into the jar; there should be enough to completely cover the lemons. Stir and poke mixture with a wooden spoon handle to ensure there are no air bubbles in the jars. Seal the jars, shaking to distribute the contents, and then leave in a sunny place for 2 weeks. Turn jars upside down briefly once a day if possible to distribute the contents evenly. After 2 weeks, store lemons in a cool, dry place; they will keep for up to a year unopened. Once opened, they must be refrigerated.

To use the lemons, rinse thoroughly in cold water to remove the excess salt. Discard pulp and use the rinds.

Pickled Eggplants

This is one for garlic lovers! These Middle Eastern delicacies are delicious with cold meats. Always use the smallest eggplants you can find, making sure they are unblemished, firm, glossy, and as fresh as possible. Vary the spicing if you prefer them hotter.

pareve, kosher for Passover

MAKES 4 QUARTS

2 pounds very small eggplants	*2 bay leaves*
3 quarts water	*10 white peppercorns*
2 tablespoons coarse (kosher) salt	*1 tablespoon allspice berries*
2 lemons, quartered	*4 small red or green chilies*
about 12 cloves garlic	*1 cup distilled white vinegar*
2 white or yellow onions, sliced	*1 tablespoon sugar*

Remove the stems from the eggplants, being careful not to tear the skins. Place 2 quarts water, salt, and lemons in a large pot and bring to a boil over high heat. Add the eggplants and parboil them for 10 minutes, adding more water to cover the eggplants, if necessary. Remove and drain, then cut a slit in the center of each eggplant. Insert a garlic clove in each slit.

Pour remaining 1-quart water into a 3-quart enamel or stainless-steel pan, and add the onions, bay leaves, peppercorns, allspice berries, chilies, vinegar, and sugar. Bring to a boil over high heat, then add the eggplants. Turn off the heat, and let the eggplants cool to room temperature in the liquid. When cold, place the eggplants in four 1-quart canning jars, covering them with the pickling liquid and dividing the spices equally among the jars. Close and refrigerate. Serve after 3 days; keeps 3 weeks in the refrigerator.

Pickled Turnips

These pickles are typically North African. If you see a jar of red pickled turnips in the window of a little café in Israel, you can be sure the owner is from Morocco, Algeria, or Tunisia. The beets give a vivid hue to the pickles, which could become discolored during pickling. Other vegetables, such as baby eggplants, cauliflower florets, or eggs, are pickled in the same way. Always choose small, very fresh vegetables.

pareve, kosher for Passover

MAKES FOUR ½-PINTS

1 pound small, juicy turnips, trimmed and halved lengthwise
1 fresh beet
12 allspice berries

4 cloves garlic, unpeeled
6 coriander seeds
2½ cups water
4 tablespoons coarse (kosher) salt

Have ready 4 sterilized ½-pint canning jars with rings and lids. Distribute the turnips and spices among the jars. Pour water into a saucepan and add the salt. Bring the brine to a boil over high heat, then pour it over the turnips. Make sure the turnips are completely submerged in the brine; poke out any air bubbles. Close the jars and leave in a sunny place for 2 weeks, turning jars upside down briefly daily to distribute the contents. Then store jars in a cool, dark place. Pickled turnips will keep for a year, but must be refrigerated once opened.

✡

Israeli Pickled Olives

In the Middle East, olives are not mere cocktail nibbles; they are an important source of protein. During the Siege of Jerusalem in the 1948 War of Independence, hungry Israelis told each other that "ten olives are equal to one egg." Black bread and olives, with perhaps some low-fat cottage cheese, are the standard snack lunch—and they are a lot more healthful than hamburgers!

Why not try pickling your own olives? It is very rewarding, and the Israeli method brings out the true flavor of the fruits—much tastier than those bland, waterlogged canned California olives. Pickled olives take a long time to mature, but it is worth it. They are ready when they have lost their bitterness.

pareve, kosher for Passover

MAKES 4 QUARTS

2 pounds green olives, carefully cleaned
6 cups water
½ cup coarse (kosher) salt
4 bay leaves
10 black peppercorns
10 cloves garlic

4 green chilies, sliced
4 lemons, sliced
1 tablespoon paprika
2 cups olive leaves or bay leaves
olive oil

Hit each olive with a mallet or meat-hammer to crack it open. Soak the olives in a large earthenware crock or pot in water to cover, changing the water daily, for 7 days. Place water, salt, bay leaves, peppercorns, garlic, chilies, lemon slices, paprika, and leaves in a pot. Bring to a boil over high heat, then immediately remove from the heat. Let cool to room temperature, then drain, reserving the marinade ingredients.

Drain the olives and transfer to four 1-quart canning jars. Distribute marinade ingredients evenly among the jars and pour marinade liquid over. The liquid must cover the olives; if not, add more brine cooled to room temperature. (You could use the liquid from another jar of pickles, for instance.) Do not close the jars, but cover the tops lightly with cheesecloth and leave them in a cool, dark place for 1 month. Once a week, skim off the scum that will form on the brine. Top up the brine when necessary to make sure the olives are covered, using brine from another jar of pickles or by boiling and cooling 1 tablespoon coarse (kosher) salt with 1 pint water.

After 1 month, taste an olive to see if it is ready. If not, continue pickling for up to another 2 months. When the olives are ready, pour a thin film of olive oil into the top of each jar, then close with lids. Store in a cool place. They will keep for 6 months.

Yemenite Relish

This red-hot relish, called *sekhoog*, is traditional in Yemen, but has also become a favorite throughout Israel, much as Tabasco has in the United States. The color varies, as do the proportions of ingredients, since like so many popular dishes there are many variations. This version is bright green, the *sekhoog* I was served once at Kibbutz Yotvata.

If you grind the hot spices in a coffee grinder, clean the grinder thoroughly before using it for coffee again! Wear rubber gloves when making this relish, and do not touch your eyes with your hands.

pareve, kosher for Passover

MAKES ABOUT 2 CUPS

2 cardamom pods
1 teaspoon salt
1 tablespoon cumin seeds
1 tablespoon coriander seeds
2 tablespoons fenugreek seeds

6 cloves garlic
6 small green chilies
1 cup chopped fresh coriander (cilantro)
4 large green tomatoes, coarsely chopped

Have ready two ½-pint canning jars, rings, and lids. Remove the seeds from the cardamom pods. Grind them, along with the salt, cumin, coriander, and fenugreek seeds, in a spice grinder, coffee grinder, or pestle and mortar.

Puree the garlic with the chilies and coriander in a food processor. Add the tomatoes while the machine is still running and blend well. Combine tomato mixture with the spices and place in a small pan. Bring to a boil over high heat, then cool to room temperature. Pour the mixture in the jars. Seal the jars and place in a water bath. Bring the water to a boil and boil for 15 minutes. Cool and store in a cool, dark place. This paste keeps indefinitely.

Ashkenazic Charoset

Charoset is a delicious mixture that features in the Passover meal, the Seder. It symbolizes the mortar the Hebrew slaves used to bind the stones and bricks in their forced labor. Charoset is always a mixture of local fresh and dried fruits, moistened with sweet kosher wine. This is the charoset my Polish grandmother brought to our Seder table.

pareve, kosher for Passover

MAKES 1 CUP

1 large sweet apple	1 teaspoon ground cinnamon
½ cup mixed shelled nuts (almonds, walnuts, cashews, and pecans)	½ teaspoon ground allspice
	about 2 tablespoons sweet red wine

Peel and core the apple, then grate it. Grind the nuts. In a bowl, combine the grated apple and nuts, then add the spices. Stir in the wine; the mixture should have the consistency of a paste. If it is too liquid, add some more grated apple. Put it in a small bowl and place it on the Seder table.

✡

Yemenite Charoset

The peppery flavor of this charoset is typically Yemenite. Other Middle Eastern communities—the Iraqis and Persians, for instance—use the same fruits to make charoset but they omit the red pepper and substitute ground cinnamon and ground cardamom. Kurdish Jews add grated quince to the mixture.

pareve, kosher for Passover

MAKES ABOUT 1 CUP

1 cup chopped dates	1 teaspoon ground ginger
½ cup chopped figs	1 tablespoon sugar
½ cup shelled walnuts	2 tablespoons sweet red wine
1 teaspoon cayenne pepper	

In a blender or food processor, puree the dates and figs with the walnuts. Stir in the spices and sugar, and adjust the seasoning if necessary. Moisten with the wine to make a thick paste.

Chrein

This word simply means *horseradish* in Russian. To Jews, however, it represents the beet-colored horseradish condiment that is served with fish, whether fried or gefilte. Another Passover specialty, chrein is best made a couple of months before the festival. Fresh horseradish root is available year round from Chinese markets. Wear rubber gloves when handling the horseradish, and don't touch your eyes. Because this is a very strong condiment, use only a little at each meal, and store remainder in small jars in the refrigerator.

pareve, kosher for Passover

MAKES ABOUT 1½ QUARTS

2 large or 4 small cooked beets　　　*1 teaspoon salt*
2 horseradish roots, about 4 inches long　　*about 2 cups wine or cider vinegar*
1 tablespoon brown sugar or honey

Peel and grate the beets and the horseradish. (Grate the horseradish on the grating attachment of a food processor because, like onions, it causes tearing.)

Combine the beets and horseradish in a bowl, and stir in the brown sugar or honey and salt. Gradually add the vinegar; the mixture should be fairly liquid. Store in small, sterilized jars with tight-fitting lids.

Creamed Horseradish

This is a very tasty, milder mixture of chrein, used with dairy dishes.

dairy, kosher for Passover.

MAKES 1½ CUPS

1 piece horseradish root, about 2 inches　　*1 teaspoon sugar*
　long　　　　　　　　　　　　　　*about ½ cup wine vinegar*
1 tart apple　　　　　　　　　　　*⅔ cup sour cream*

Peel the horseradish and apple, then grate them together into a bowl. Stir in the sugar and just enough vinegar to moisten. Add the sour cream and blend well. Store in sterilized jars in refrigerator or until needed.

Sweet Beet Preserve

Beets are the most Jewish of vegetables, since they feature in the cooking of almost every community. The tops are used as greens, and the red root for coloring and flavoring a wide variety of dishes. This delicious relish is, like most European beet products, associated with Passover. Make it about 3 months before the festival, so the pickle has time to mature.

pareve, kosher for Passover

MAKES 8 QUARTS

4 pounds fresh beets	*2 inches fresh ginger root, peeled and*
2½ quarts water	*grated*
7 cups sugar	*½ cup chopped walnuts or pecans*
juice of 6 lemons	*½ cup chopped blanched almonds*

Place the beets in a large saucepan. Cover with water and bring to a boil over high heat. Reduce heat and cook beets for 20 minutes, or until tender. Drain well.

Peel the beets and slice into matchstick strips or grate them on a coarse grater. Put beet slivers into a large enamel or stainless-steel pot with the water, sugar, lemon juice, and ginger root. Stir well with a wooden spoon until the sugar has dissolved, and bring to a boil over high heat. Reduce the heat slightly and cook, uncovered, at a gentle boil for 2 hours or until the mixture is thick.

Add the nuts to the beets. Stir well, and cook for 15 minutes. Begin testing for doneness by dropping a little of the mixture onto a cold saucer. if it starts to jell, mixture is ready. Wash and sterilize eight 1-quart canning jars, rings, and new lids. Fill them with the preserve to within ½ inch of the top. Put the jars in a water bath, and bring the water to a boil. Process 30 minutes, then cool. Store in a cool, dark place.

CONVERSION TABLE

SOLID MEASURES

For cooks measuring items by weight, here are approximate equivalents, in both Imperial and metric. So as to avoid awkward measurements, some conversions are not exact.

	U.S. CUSTOMARY	METRIC	IMPERIAL
Butter	1 cup	225 g	8 oz
	½ cup	115 g	4 oz
	¼ cup	60 g	2 oz
	1 Tbsp	15 g	½ oz
Cheese (grated)	1 cup	115 g	4 oz
Fruit (chopped fresh)	1 cup	225 g	8 oz
Herbs (chopped fresh)	¼ cup	7 g	¼ oz
Meats/Chicken (chopped, cooked)	1 cup	175 g	6 oz
Mushrooms (chopped, fresh)	1 cup	70 g	2½ oz
Nuts (chopped)	1 cup	115 g	4 oz
Raisins (and other dried chopped fruits)	1 cup	175 g	6 oz
Rice (uncooked)	1 cup	225 g	8 oz
(cooked)	3 cups	225 g	8 oz
Vegetables (chopped, raw)	1 cup	115 g	4 oz

LIQUID MEASURES

The Imperial pint is larger than the U.S. pint; therefore, note the following when measuring liquid ingredients.

U.S.	IMPERIAL
1 cup = 8 fluid ounces	1 cup = 10 fluid ounces
½ cup = 4 fluid ounces	½ cup = 5 fluid ounces
1 tablespoon = ¾ fluid ounce	1 tablespoon = 1 fluid ounce

U.S. MEASURE	METRIC APPROXIMATE	IMPERIAL APPROXIMATE
1 quart (4 cups)	950 mL	1½ pints + 4 Tbsp
1 pint (2 cups)	450 mL	¾ pint
1 cup	236 mL	¼ pint + 6 Tbsp
1 Tbsp	15 mL	1+ Tbsp
1 tsp	5mL	1 tsp

DRY MEASURES

Outside the United States, the following items are measured by weight. Use the following table, but bear in mind that measurements will vary, depending on the variety of flour and moisture. Cup measurements are loosely packed; flour is measured directly from package (presifted).

	U.S. CUSTOMARY	METRIC	IMPERIAL
Flour (all-purpose)	1 cup	150 g	5 oz
Cornmeal	1 cup	175 g	6 oz
Sugar (granulated)	1 cup	190 g	6½ oz
(confectioners)	1 cup	80 g	2⅔ oz
(brown)	1 cup	160 g	5⅓ oz

OVEN TEMPERATURES

Fahrenheit	225	300	350	400	450
Celsius	110	150	180	200	230
Gas Mark	¼	2	4	6	8

INDEX